THE
PASSION
TRANSLATION

Mark

MIRACLES AND MERCY

Translated from Greek and Aramaic Texts

DR. BRIAN SIMMONS

tPt
BIBLE

BroadStreet
PUBLISHING

Mark: Miracles and Mercy, The Passion Translation®

Translated directly from Greek and Aramaic texts by Dr. Brian Simmons

Published by BroadStreet Publishing Group, LLC
Racine, Wisconsin, USA
BroadStreetPublishing.com

© 2015 The Passion Translation

ISBN-13: 978-1-4245-4969-6 (paperback)
ISBN-13: 978-1-4245-4970-2 (e-book)

Cover and interior design by Chris Garborg at garborgdesign.com
Interior typesetting by Katherine Lloyd at theDESKonline.com

Printed in the United States of America
16 17 18 19 20   10 9 8 7 6 5 4 3 2

Translator's Introduction to Mark

AT A GLANCE

Author: John Mark

Audience: Roman Christians

Date: AD 50–55

Type of Literature: Ancient historical biography

Major Themes: The person of Jesus, the mission of Jesus, the work of Jesus, discipleship and faith, the kingdom realm.

Outline:
   Prologue — 1:1–13
   Jesus' Galilee Ministry: Phase 1 — 1:14–3:6
   Jesus' Galilee Ministry: Phase 2 — 3:7–6:13
   Jesus Leaves Galilee — 6:14–8:21
   Jesus Journeys to Jerusalem — 8:22–10:52
   Jesus' Jerusalem Ministry — 11:1–13:37
   Jesus' Passion — 14:1–15:47
   Jesus' Resurrection — 16:1–8 (9–20)

ABOUT MARK

God has given the world a treasure with the gospel of Mark! What a beautiful description we find of Jesus, the Anointed One, within its pages. Mark unveils the Lord Jesus before our eyes as the true Servant of God, holy, harmless, and merciful! As God's Servant we find Jesus very busy in this gospel healing, teaching, and working wonders. You will fall in love with Jesus Christ as you read this inspired account of his life.

Many believe Mark was a disciple of Peter and received much of the material given in his gospel from Peter, for Peter describes Mark as "my son" (1 Peter 5:13). The church fathers Papias and Clement of Alexandria both state that Mark wrote a factual and inspired gospel with the help of Peter while Peter was still living. We know for sure that Mark wrote under the inspiration of the Holy Spirit and gave us a vibrant, striking picture of the life of the Messiah, Jesus, the Servant of the Lord. It is likely that Mark wrote this gospel about AD 50–55. The book easily divides itself between Jesus' Galilean ministry (1:1-8:21) and his Judean ministry (8:22-16:8).

Mark omits the narrative of Jesus' birth and genealogy, for a servant needs no pedigree. But rather, he introduces Jesus as the one with a mission of love and power to change the world. Forty times Mark uses the Greek word *eutheos*, which means "immediately"! There is urgency with Jesus as he works toward completing his task of providing salvation and power to all who believe in him.

Mark records nearly three times as many miracles as parables. This is a gospel of miracles! Eighteen miracles are recorded here with two unique to Mark's gospel. There is a freshness and vitality about this gospel that is gripping to the reader. See if you can read the entire gospel through in one sitting—you'll be on the edge of your seat! Although it is the briefest of the four gospels, you'll still enjoy reading about Jesus' supreme power over both the invisible and visible worlds. He was with the wild beasts in the wilderness and subdued the even wilder nature of demon-controlled souls. He is Master over creation, man, and the devil, for he is the perfect servant who came to do the Father's will.

Mercy triumphs in every page of Mark's gospel, for he writes as one set free from his past and as one who has discovered the divine surprise of mercy. May you also find mercy triumphant as you read the translation of this book. Today is the day for you to become a fervent follower of the Lord Jesus Christ!

PURPOSE

While John Mark likely had a variety of reasons for writing his gospel, two broad themes stand out: 1) to confirm Jesus' messianic identity; and 2) to call believers to follow Jesus' example. The first purpose is confirmed by the dramatic middle where Peter confesses, "You are the Messiah, the Son of the Living God!" The whole story pivots around this confirmation, though Jesus won't be confined to anyone's definition. Because while Peter and Israel expected a conquering hero Messiah, Jesus is the Suffering Servant Messiah. It is through the cross he achieves his full glory and full identity!

In his second purpose, Mark builds on his first by exhorting believers to follow Jesus' example. The disciples aren't the ones we are to model, however, for they repeatedly fail and remain relatively faithless throughout; their example is one to avoid! Instead, we are to pattern our lives after Jesus' own faithful, cross-shaped life. As Jesus said, "If you truly want to follow me, you should at once completely disown your own life. And you must be willing to share my cross and experience it as your own" (Mark 8:34).

AUTHOR AND AUDIENCE

The author of the gospel of Mark is nearly universally recognized to be the John Mark who was related to Barnabas and lived in Jerusalem (Acts 12:12). He and Barnabas and Paul once traveled together in their missionary work (Acts 13:4) until some kind of failure took place in Mark's life and he left his team for a short period. Because of his abrupt departure, Paul refused to have Mark rejoin them from that time forward, which caused a rift between Paul and Barnabas. Even so, Barnabas the encourager still took Mark with him to advance the work of the gospel (Acts 15:36-39). It is also likely that Mark is the individual he mentions in Mark 14:51, using the common literary tool of that day when speaking of oneself by allusion.

Isn't it amazing how God does not give up on us because of our failures? It is comforting to see how God's mercy restored Mark and used him to write this inspired record, a gospel that will endure for all eternity. Later, while Paul was imprisoned, he asked Timothy to bring Mark to him, saying, "For he (Mark) is a tremendous help for me in my ministry" (2 Timothy 4:11). So we learn that none of our failures need disqualify us if we continue to love and follow Jesus Christ. When you get to heaven, ask Mark. He will tell you that mercy triumphs over judgment!

While the Gospels were written for the church at large, the writers often had specific audiences in mind and addressed needs and concerns relevant to them. Early Christian tradition closely identifies Mark's gospel with Rome. This is supported by church fathers like Irenaeus and Clement of Alexandria. Since Mark translates Aramaic words into Greek for his readers and explains Jewish customs, a Palestinian audience seems to be ruled out. And because he uses Roman words in place of Greek ones, Christians in Rome were a likely target audience. He wrote to these Roman Christians to bring encouragement and assurance in their faith.

MAJOR THEMES

The Person of Jesus

Mark wrote his gospel to write Jesus' story; the unfolding story itself reveals who Jesus is. He clues us into the revelation of his Person in the opening stanza: "This is the beginning of the wonderful news about Jesus the Messiah, the Son of God." These two titles, Messiah and Son of God, point to what Jesus has come to do, which is key to understanding who Jesus is: He is the bearer of God's salvation, announced in words and deeds, teaching and miracles, and ultimately his sacrifice!

The Messianic Mission of Jesus

One of the most peculiar aspects of Mark's gospel is the so-called "Messianic Secret." At various times Jesus commands his disciples not to reveal his true messianic identity. He tells others whom he's healed to keep his identity a secret too. In fact, the demons are commanded to keep the secret! Though he clearly demonstrated his identity through his miracle and teaching ministry, his full identity as Israel's awaited Messiah wouldn't be revealed until the end when he was resurrected in full glory.

The Work of Jesus

Some have said Mark is a passion narrative with a lengthy introduction. Perhaps this is a bit of an overstatement, but Jesus' death plays a central role in this gospel. While the work of Christ on the cross doesn't appear until the fourteenth chapter, Mark peppers references to Jesus' crucifixion throughout. He wrote to show that Jesus' death on the cross wasn't a tragedy or mistake, but God's plan from the beginning. Through suffering and death Jesus brings in the last days of God's kingdom realm. Through the crucifixion we see Jesus was both the long-awaited Messiah as well as the Son of God, which comes through the climactic confession of the Roman centurion: "There is no doubt, this man was the Son of God!" (Mark 15:39).

Discipleship and Faith

At every turn in Mark's gospel, Jesus is inviting people to follow him. This is the essence of discipleship. It's an invitation extended to everyone and anyone. Jesus taught that this kind of following involves three things: self-denial, cross bearing, and daily living. Denying oneself is about submitting to the lordship of Christ over every ounce of one's life. Taking up one's cross reminds us of Jesus' own self-denial on that cross of execution and committing himself fully to God's will; it is a radical and total commitment. Finally, following Jesus is a continuous, daily act that requires living out Jesus' teachings and example. This relationship is built on faith, which isn't some magical formula, but a repeated hearing of Jesus' teachings and participation in his way of life.

The Kingdom Realm of God

"It is time for the realm of God's kingdom to be experienced in its fullness!" Jesus announced at the beginning of his ministry. "Turn your lives back to God and put your trust in the hope-filled gospel!" As with the other Gospels, God's kingdom realm takes center stage in Mark from the beginning where this opening stanza summarizes the good news Jesus brought. Later, in chapter four, Mark summarizes the entire ministry of Jesus and its effects with this term. The world is brought under "God's kingship" in and through the work of Jesus. For Mark the kingdom realm is already dynamically in the present, yet fully experienced in the future. It's surprising and small, yet powerful and great; beyond understanding for many, yet accessible for all; and calls people to a radical new way of living and challenges every human value.

A WORD ABOUT THE PASSION TRANSLATION

The message of God's story is timeless; the Word of God doesn't change. But the methods by which that story is communicated should be timely; the vessels that steward God's Word can and should change.

One of those timely methods and vessels is Bible translations. However, there is no such thing as a truly literal translation of the Bible, for there is not an equivalent language that perfectly conveys the meaning of the biblical text except as it is understood in its original cultural and linguistic setting. So it is important that a translator seeks to transfer meaning, and not merely words, from the original text to the receptor language.

The goal of The Passion Translation is to reintroduce the passion and fire of the original, life-changing message of God's Word for modern readers—not merely to convey the original, literal meaning of words, but also to express God's passion for people and his world.

Italicized Words and Hebrew Names

You will notice at times we've italicized certain words or phrases. These highlighted portions are not in the original Hebrew, Aramaic, and Greek manuscripts, but are implied from the context. We've made these implications explicit for the sake of narrative clarity and to better convey the meaning of God's Word. This is a common practice by mainstream translations, including the New American Standard Bible and King James Version.

We've also chosen to translate certain names in their original Hebrew or Greek form to better convey their cultural meaning and significance. For instance, it is unfortunate that translations of the Bible have substituted Miriam with Mary and Jacob with James. Both Greek and Aramaic leave the Hebrew names in their original form. Therefore this translation uses their correct cultural names, Miriam and Jacob, throughout.

God longs to have his Word expressed in every language in a way that would unlock the passion of his heart. Our goal is to trigger inside every English speaker an overwhelming response to the truth of the Bible. This is a heart-level translation, from the passion of God's heart to the passion of your heart.

We pray and trust this version of God's Word will kindle in you a burning, passionate desire for him and his heart, while impacting the church for years to come!

$\mathcal{O}ne$

___

The Wonderful News

¹This is the beginning of the wonderful news about Jesus[a] the Messiah, the Son of God.[b]

²It starts with Isaiah the prophet, who wrote:

> **Listen! I am sending my messenger ahead of you[c]**
> **and he will prepare your way!**
> ³**He is a thunderous voice of one**
> **who shouts in the wilderness:**
> **"Prepare your hearts[d]**
> **for the coming of the Lord Yahweh,[e]**
> **and clear a straight path**
> **inside your hearts for him!"[f]**

___

a 1:1 The Aramaic is "the revelation of Jesus."
b 1:1 Although the words "Son of God" are missing from some Greek manuscripts, it is found in the Aramaic.
c 1:2 This line is a quotation from Exodus 23:20 and Malachi 3:1, where it is an "angel (messenger)" that God sends before them.
d 1:3 Or "Prepare the way for the Lord and make his beaten paths straight, level, and passable." This "way" is not a road, but preparing the heart, making room for the ways of the Lord.
e 1:3 As translated from the Aramaic.
f 1:3 See Isaiah 40:3.

[4]John the Immerser[a] was the messenger who appeared in an uninhabited region, preaching a baptism of repentance[b] for the complete cancellation of sins. [5]A steady stream of people came to be dipped in the Jordan River as they publicly confessed their sins. They came from all over southern Israel,[c] including nearly all the inhabitants of Jerusalem. [6]John wore a rough garment made from camel hair,[d] with a leather belt around his waist,[e] and he ate locusts and honey of the wilderness. [7]And this is the message he kept preaching: "There is a man coming after me who is greater and a lot more powerful than I am. I'm not even worthy to bend down and untie the strap of his sandals. [8]I've buried you into water, but he will bury you into the Spirit of Holiness!"

The Baptism and Testing of Jesus

[9]One day, Jesus came from the Galilean village of Nazareth[f] and had John immerse him in the Jordan River. [10]The moment Jesus rose

---

a 1:4 John was the son of Zechariah, a priest. As the son of a priest, John was qualified to serve in the temple but chose instead the lonely wilderness to begin his ministry of calling a nation to repentance and preparing the way for the Lord Jesus.

b 1:4 That is, "an immersion that will bring a change of heart and lead you into repentance for the complete cancellation of sins."

c 1:5 Or "Judea."

d 1:6 John was not afraid to violate religious taboos. A camel was considered unclean in the Jewish tradition. He was wearing what others considered to be unclean. Those who break loose of religious tradition will often appear to be undignified, as was John. His commission was to inaugurate a new way of living according to the truths of Jesus Christ and the Holy Spirit.

e 1:6 This was considered to be the wardrobe of a prophet and was identical to what the prophet Elijah wore (2 Kings 1:8 and Zechariah 13:4). With a diet of locusts John points back to the four varieties of locusts mentioned in Joel 1:4. Locusts (grasshoppers) are an emblem of intimidation that will keep believers from taking their inheritance by faith. Israel thought of themselves to be like grasshoppers in their own eyes because of the intimidation of the fierce inhabitants of the land. John the Immerser arrives on the scene and makes locusts his food, eating up that symbol of intimidation (devouring the devourer). And he drank honey, which is a biblical metaphor for the revelation of God's Word that is sweeter than honey (Psalm 19:7–10). John's ministry was a prophetic statement from God that a new day had come, a day of leaving dead formalism and embracing new life in Jesus without intimidation.

f 1:9 It is possible to translate the Aramaic as "Then one day Jesus came from Victorious Revelation" to be baptized by John. The word Nazareth can mean "victorious one," and the word Galilee can be translated "the place of revelation."

up out of the water, John saw the heavenly realm split open, and the Holy Spirit descended like a dove and rested upon him.[a] [11]At the same time, a voice spoke from heaven, saying:

> **"You are my Son, my cherished one,**
> **and my greatest delight is in you!"[b]**

[12]Immediately after this he was compelled by the Holy Spirit[c] to go into an uninhabited desert region. [13]He remained there in the wilderness for forty days,[d] enduring the ordeals of Satan's tests. He encountered wild animals, but also angels who appeared and ministered to his needs.[e]

Jesus Calls Four Fishermen to Follow Him

[14]Later on, after John the Immerser was arrested, Jesus went back into the region of Galilee and preached the wonderful gospel of God's kingdom realm.[f] [15]His message was this: **"At last the fulfillment of the age has come! It is time for the realm of God's kingdom to be experienced in its fullness! Turn your lives back to God and put your trust in the hope-filled gospel!"[g]**

---

a 1:10 The Lord Jesus was buried in baptism, symbolically into death (Jordan) so that he might minister not in the natural way of men, but in the way of resurrection by the power of the Holy Spirit. The dove, an emblem of the Holy Spirit, pictures both meekness and purity. The implication is that the Holy Spirit came upon Jesus and never left him.

b 1:11 Although not a direct quotation, the wording is similar to Psalm 2:7.

c 1:12 Or "cast out (thrown, or pushed) into the wilderness." The Greek word *ekballei* is often used for driving out demons. This was a forceful compelling of the Holy Spirit.

d 1:13 The "forty days" points to Moses, Elijah, and David, who were all great champions in Israel's history. See Exodus 34:28, 1 Kings 19:8, 15, and 1 Samuel 17:16.

e 1:13 Between verses 13 and 14 there is an entire year of our Lord's life that Mark skips over. Jesus spent most of that year in and around Jerusalem. The gospel of John gives further details of that year in chapter 1.

f 1:14 As translated from the Aramaic and most Greek manuscripts.

g 1:15 The Greek is "Believe the good news (the gospel)," and the Aramaic is "Put your trust in the joyful message of hope." This translation merges both concepts, making it *"the hope-filled gospel."*

¹⁶As Jesus was walking along the shore of the Lake of Galilee, he noticed two brothers fishing: Simon and Andrew. He watched them as they were casting their nets into the sea ¹⁷and said to them, **"Come follow me and I will transform you into men who catch people instead of fish!"**[a] ¹⁸Immediately they dropped their nets and left everything behind to follow Jesus. ¹⁹Walking a little farther, Jesus found two other brothers sitting in a boat, along with their father, mending their nets. Their names were Jacob[b] and John, and their father Zebedee.[c] ²⁰Jesus immediately walked up to them and invited the two brothers to become his followers. At once, Jacob[d] and John dropped their nets, stood up, left their father in the boat with the hired men, and followed Jesus.[e]

People Stunned by Jesus' Teachings

²¹Then Jesus and his disciples went to Capernaum,[f] and he immediately started teaching on the Sabbath day in the synagogue. ²²The

---

a 1:17 The metaphor of "fishers of men" simply means that they will persuade others and catch people for God.

b 1:19 Or "James." It is unfortunate that other translations of the Bible have substituted Jacob for James. Both Greek and Aramaic leave the Hebrew name as it is, Jacob. This translation will use the correct name, Jacob, throughout.

c 1:19 Zebedee means "my gift." Zebedee's gift to Jesus was his sons. A wise father will always want his children to be given to Jesus.

d 1:20 Or "James."

e 1:20 What a powerful effect Jesus had upon people! One encounter with the Son of God compelled these businessmen to leave their trade and follow Jesus. We learn from Luke 5:10 that the family of Zebedee was in business together with Simon (Peter) and Andrew. They owned the boat and had a hired crew, which makes one think they were somewhat prosperous business owners, for commercial fishermen in the time of Jesus were usually wealthy.

f 1:21 Capernaum means "the village of Nahum." Nahum means "comforted." Jesus did many miracles and made his Galilean base of ministry in "the village of the comforted."

people were awestruck and overwhelmed[a] by his teaching, because he taught in a way that demonstrated *God's* authority, which was quite unlike the religious scholars.[b]

²³Suddenly, during the meeting, a demon-possessed man screamed out, ²⁴"Hey! Leave us alone! Jesus the Victorious,[c] I know who you are. You're God's Holy One and you have come to destroy us!"[d]

²⁵Jesus rebuked him, saying, **"Silence! You are bound![e] Come out of him!"**

²⁶The man's body shook violently in spasms, and the demon hurled him to the floor until it finally came out of him with a deafening shriek! ²⁷The crowd was awestruck and unable to stop saying among themselves, "What is this new teaching that comes with such authority? With merely a word he commands demons to come out and they obey him!"

²⁸So the reports about Jesus spread like wildfire throughout every community in the region of Galilee.

---

a 1:22 The Greek word used here, *ekplesso*, is a strong verb that means "awestruck, filled with amazement, astonished, panic stricken, something that takes your breath away (being hit with a blow), to be shocked, to expel, to drive out." Clearly, Jesus spoke with such glory and power emanating from him that his words were like thunderbolts in their hearts. May we hear his words in the same way today.

b 1:22 Or "scribes (experts of the Law)." Jesus taught from an inner knowledge of God and his Word, for his teaching emphasized obedience to God from the heart, not just outwardly keeping of laws.

c 1:24 As translated from the Aramaic. The Greek is "Jesus the Nazarene (Branch or Scion)."

d 1:24 The demon knew Jesus' true identity before the people did. This is not so much a question (Have you come to destroy us?), but rather an assertive and defiant declaration. There is no question mark in the Greek text. The demonized man was apparently comfortable in the presence of the religious teachers, but when Jesus stepped into the room, he spoke out and couldn't resist the power of Jesus.

e 1:25 Or "muzzled."

Jesus Heals Many

²⁹Now, as soon as they left the meeting, they went straight to Simon and Andrew's house, along with Jacob[a] and John. ³⁰Simon's mother-in-law was bedridden, sick with a high fever, so the first thing they did was to tell Jesus about her. ³¹He walked up to her bedside, gently took her hand, and raised her up! Her fever disappeared and she began to serve them.

³²Later in the day, *just after the Sabbath ended*[b] at sunset, the people kept bringing to Jesus all who were sick and tormented by demons, ³³until the whole village was crowded around the house. ³⁴Jesus instantly healed those who suffered severely from various diseases[c] and cast out many demons. But he would not permit the demons to speak, because they knew who he really was.[d]

Jesus Prays, Preaches, Heals, and Casts Out Demons

³⁵The next morning, Jesus got up long before daylight, left the house while it was dark, and made his way to a secluded place to give himself to prayer. ³⁶Later, Simon and his friends searched for him, ³⁷and when they finally tracked him down, they told him, "Everyone is looking for you—they want you!"

³⁸Jesus replied, **"We have to go on to the surrounding villages so that I can give my message to the people there, for that is my mission."** ³⁹So he went throughout the region of Galilee, preaching in the Jewish synagogues and casting out demons.

---

a 1:29 Or "James."

b 1:32 Implied in the context.

c 1:34 The Greek word *kakos* is actually the word for "evil"; however, it is traditionally translated "sickness."

d 1:34 Jesus wants *us* to proclaim who he is, not demons.

⁴⁰On one occasion, a leper came and threw himself down in front of Jesus, pleading for his healing, saying, "You have the power to heal me right now if only you really want to!" ⁴¹Being deeply moved with tender compassion,[a] Jesus reached out and touched the skin of the leper and told him, **"Of course I want you to be healed—so now, be cleansed!"** ⁴²Instantly his leprous sores completely disappeared and his skin became smooth! ⁴³Jesus sent him away with a very stern warning,[b] ⁴⁴saying, **"Don't say anything to anyone** *about what just happened,* **but go find a priest and show him that you've been healed. Then bring the offering that Moses commanded for your cleansing as a living testimony to everyone."**[c]

⁴⁵But no sooner did the man leave than he began to proclaim his healing publicly[d] and spread the story everywhere *of his healing.*

Jesus' growing fame prevented him from entering the villages openly, which forced him to remain in isolated places. Even so, a steady stream of people flocked to him from everywhere.

---

a 1:41 This is an intense emotion. Some Greek manuscripts have, "Jesus was moved with anger (at the leprosy, not the man)." However, the Aramaic is clearly "moved with compassion." The two Aramaic words for "anger" and "compassion" are written almost identically. Perhaps both are correct. Jesus was deeply moved with compassion toward the man and angry at the disease.

b 1:43 The Greek word *embrimaomai* can mean "to sternly give a warning"; however, in John 11:33 it is translated "to be deeply and intensely moved in spirit." The miracle of healing this leper had a profound effect on both Jesus and the man who was healed.

c 1:44 See Leviticus 14:1–32. Normally, touching a leper would make a man unclean, but in this instance, the leper was healed and Jesus was not defiled.

d 1:45 Or "preach."

Two

Jesus Heals a Paralyzed Man

¹Several days later, Jesus returned to Capernaum, and the news quickly spread that he was back in town. ²Soon there were so many people crowded inside the house to hear him that there was no more room, even outside the door.

While Jesus was preaching the word of God, ³four men arrived, carrying a paralyzed man. ⁴But when they realized that they couldn't even get near him because of the crowd, they went up on top of the house and tore away the roof above Jesus' head. And when they had broken through, they lowered the paralyzed man on a stretcher *right down in front of him*! ⁵When Jesus saw the extent of their faith, he said to the paralyzed man, **"My son, your sins are now forgiven."**

⁶This offended some of the religious scholars who were present, and they reasoned among themselves, ⁷"Who does he think he is to speak this way? This is blasphemy for sure! Only God himself can forgive sins!"

⁸Jesus supernaturally perceived their thoughts and said to them, **"Why are you being so skeptical? ⁹Which is easier, to say to this**

paralyzed man, 'Your sins are now forgiven,' or, 'Stand up and walk!'?[a] [10]But to convince you that the Son of Man has been given authority to forgive sins, [11]I say to this man, 'Stand up, pick up your stretcher, and walk home.'" [12]Immediately the man sprang to his feet in front of everyone and left for home.

When the crowds witnessed this miracle, they were awestruck.[b] They shouted praises to God and said, "We've never seen anything like this before!"

Jesus Calls Levi (Matthew) to Follow Him

[13]Jesus went out to walk near the Lake of Galilee, and a massive crowed gathered, so he taught them. [14]As he walked along, he found Levi, the son of Alphaeus,[c] sitting at the tax booth, collecting taxes. He approached him and said, **"Come follow me."** Immediately he got up from his booth and began to follow Jesus.

[15]Later, Jesus and his disciples went to have a meal with Levi. Among the guests in Levi's home were many tax collectors and notable sinners sharing a meal with Jesus, for there were many kinds of people who followed him. [16]But when the religious scholars and the Pharisees[d] found out that Jesus was keeping company

---

a 2:9 The answer to Jesus' question is obvious. It is easy for anyone to say, "Your sins are forgiven," for that cannot be proven. But if someone were to tell a paralyzed man to stand up, and he didn't stand up, that would prove the person is a fraud. Jesus didn't do the easy thing without accomplishing the hard thing, the miracle of healing. Forgiveness and healing both flow from Jesus Christ.

b 2:12 The Greek word used here can also mean "shocked into wonderment" or "to be out of their minds (with amazement)." This event teaches us that salvation not only involves the forgiveness of our sins, but gives us the power to rise up and walk.

c 2:14 The name Levi means "joined, united," and Levi is the same person as Matthew, who wrote the gospel bearing his name. Alphaeus means "changing." It is obvious that Matthew's allegiance is changing from being a servant of Rome to being joined to Jesus as his future apostle.

d 2:16 The word Pharisee means "separated one."

and dining with sinners and tax collectors,[a] they were indignant. So they approached Jesus' disciples and said to them, "Why is it that someone like Jesus *defiles himself* by eating with sinners and tax collectors?"

[17]But when Jesus overheard their complaint, he said to them, **"Who goes to the doctor for a cure? Those who are well or those who are sick? I have not come to call the 'righteous,' but to call those who are sinners and bring them to repentance."**

Jesus Questioned about Fasting

[18]One time, the disciples of John the Immerser and the Pharisees were fasting. So they came to Jesus and asked, "Why is it that John's disciples and disciples of the Pharisees are fasting but your disciples are not?"

[19]Jesus answered, **"How can the sons of the bridal chamber fast when the bridegroom is next to them? As long as the bridegroom is with them they won't, [20]but the days of fasting will come when the Bridegroom is taken from them.**

[21]**"And who would mend worn-out clothing with new fabric? When the new cloth shrinks, it will rip, making the tear worse than before. [22]And who would pour fresh, new wine into an old wineskin? Eventually the wine will ferment and make the wineskin burst, losing everything—the wine will be spilled and the wineskin ruined. Instead, new wine is always poured into new wineskins."**

---

a 2:16 These were Jews who worked for the Roman empire to collect taxes and were empowered by Rome to profit greatly by what they collected.

Jesus, Lord of the Sabbath

²³One Saturday, on the day of rest,ᵃ Jesus and his disciples were walking through a field of wheat. The disciples were hungry, so they plucked off some heads of grain to eat. ²⁴But when some of the Pharisees saw what was happening, they said to him, "Look! Your disciples shouldn't be harvesting grain on the Sabbath!"

²⁵Jesus responded, **"Haven't you ever read what King David and his men did when they were hungry? ²⁶They entered the house of God**ᵇ **when Abiathar was high priest and ate the sacred bread of God's presence.**ᶜ **They violated the law by eating bread that only the priests were allowed to eat. But there is one here who is even greater than the temple."**

²⁷Then he said to them, **"The Sabbath was made for the sake of people, and not people for the Sabbath. ²⁸For this reason the Son of Man exercises his lordship over the Sabbath."**

---

a 2:23 Or "Sabbath." The Hebrew word for Sabbath comes from *shavat*, which is the verb "to rest." What was designed to be a day of rest and intimacy with God and family was now complicated by a host of rules and traditions.

b 2:26 That is, the tabernacle. See 1 Samuel 21:1–6. Ancient Jewish tradition states that David did this on a Sabbath day. See also Leviticus 24:5–9.

c 2:26 Or "loaves of presentation." See Ezekiel 44:15–16.

$$Three$$

Jesus Heals on the Sabbath

¹Then Jesus left them and went again into the synagogue, where he encountered a man who had an atrophied, paralyzed hand. ²Everyone was watching Jesus closely to see if he would heal the man on the Sabbath, giving them a reason to accuse him *of breaking Sabbath rules.*

³Jesus said to the man with the paralyzed hand, **"Stand here in the middle of the room."**

⁴Then he turned to all those gathered there and said, **"Which is it? Is it against the law to do evil on the Sabbath or to do good? To destroy a life or to save one?"** But no one answered him a word.

⁵Then looking around at everyone, Jesus was moved with indignation and grieved by the hardness of their hearts and said to the man, **"Now stretch out your hand!"** As he stretched out his hand, it was instantly healed!ᵃ

⁶After this happened, the Pharisees left abruptly and began to

---

a 3:5 This miracle is found in Matthew, Mark, and Luke. It contains valuable lessons for us today, for the hand symbolizes holding, giving, receiving, doing. It was his right hand (Luke 6:6), which brings the added significance of power (i.e., God's right hand, Exodus 15:6), pleasure (Psalm 16:11), approval (Hebrews 1:13), and righteousness (Psalm 48:10). A crippled right hand points to the lack of all these things. Human beings are helpless before God, crippled in all our works. But the power of Jesus heals our limitations and brokenness. Religion cannot heal us, but Jesus can.

plot together with the friends and supporters of Herod Antipas on how they would kill Jesus.

Massive Crowds Follow Jesus

7Once again Jesus withdrew with his disciples to the lakeside, but a massive crowd of people followed him from all around the provinces of Galilee and southern Israel. 8Vast crowds came from Jerusalem, Idumea,*a* beyond the Jordan, and from Lebanon.*b* Large numbers of people swarmed in from everywhere when they heard of him and his wonderful works.

9The crowd pressed so closely to Jesus that he instructed his disciples to bring him a small boat to get into and keep from being crushed by the crowd. 10For he had healed so many that the sick kept pushing forward*c* just so they could touch Jesus. 11And whenever a demon saw him, it would throw the person down at Jesus' feet, screaming out, "You are the Son of God!" 12But Jesus would silence the demons and sternly order them not to reveal who he was.

Jesus Chooses Twelve Apostles

13Afterward, Jesus went up on a mountainside and called to himself the men he wanted to be his close companions, so they went up the mountainside to join him. 14He appointed*d* the Twelve, whom he named apostles.*e* He wanted them to be continually at his side as his

---

a 3:8 Or "Edom." Idumea was the region south of Beersheba, south and west of the Dead Sea, a territory of ancient Israel.

b 3:8 Or "Tyre and Sidon," which are in modern-day Lebanon.

c 3:10 Or "falling all over him." Jesus had power coming through him for healing, and everyone wanted to touch him. What a wonderful Savior who loves and heals people!

d 3:14 This was not simply a passive acknowledgment, but an active setting them in place. The Greek verb *poieo* is the verb "do" or "make." Jesus "did" them; that is, he imparted his favor, blessing, and grace to set them in place as apostolic emissaries for the kingdom realm of God.

e 3:14 The Greek word *apostoles* means "sent ones."

friends, and so that he could send them out to preach [15]and have authority to heal the sick and to cast out demons.[a]

[16]He appointed his Twelve[b] and gave Simon the nickname Peter the Rock.[c] [17]And he gave the brothers, Jacob[d] and John, the sons of Zebedee, the nickname Benay-Regah,[e] which means "passionate sons." [18]The others were Andrew, Philip, Bartholomew,[f] Matthew, Thomas, Jacob[g] the son of Alphaeus, Thaddaeus,[h] Simon the Nationalist,[i] [19]and Judas Iscariot,[j] who betrayed him.

---

a 3:15 As translated from the Aramaic and a few Greek manuscripts. This ordination was for a three-fold purpose: 1) that they might continually be at his side, 2) to send them out with love for others, preaching the truth of God's Word, and 3) to receive power to heal and cast out demons. This is the same for all whom Jesus calls to represent him. See Acts 4:13.

b 3:16 These twelve disciples became apostles (sent ones), serving the God's kingdom realm. Jesus raised up twelve, and later seventy, whom he sent out to preach the message of God's kingdom. None of them were fully mature or equipped, for the Holy Spirit had not yet come to empower them. Leaders today need to raise up others and not center their ministry around themselves. The legacy of a spiritual leader is made up of those whom he or she has released and sent forth to proclaim Christ.

c 3:16 In the ancient Hebraic mind-set, to name something is to give it existence, purpose, and function. (See Genesis 32:27–28.) In the Greek mind-set, naming is simply assigning phonetic sounds to an object or a person. When Jesus gave this name to Peter the Rock, he was calling his purpose into existence. Peter would be a strong rock of faith and a leader to the other eleven apostles. Peter is always named first in all the listings of the Twelve (Matthew 10:1–4, Luke 6:13–16, and Acts 1:13). The name Jesus gave him was Keefa, the Aramaic word for "rock." The Greek is Petros, which in John 1:42 is explained as the translation from Galilean Aramaic.

d Or "James." It is unfortunate that translations of the Bible have substituted Jacob with James. Both Greek and Aramaic leave the Hebrew name as it is, Jacob. This translation will use the correct name, Jacob, throughout.

e 3:17 As translated from Aramaic. The Greek transliteration is Boanerges. Benay-Regah can also be translated "sons of loud shouts (passionate)" or "sons of commotion (easily angered)" or "sons of thunder." Jesus, by giving the brothers this nickname, acknowledged that they were two rowdy boys, thunderous and passionate. Jesus chose twelve men who were all different in their personality types. It was no doubt humorous to Jesus to observe how different these twelve men were and how difficult it was to form them into a band of brothers.

f 3:18 Or in Aramaic, "the son of Tolmai (discipline)." This could be another name for Nathaniel.

g See footnote d.

h 3:18 Or "Lebbaeus."

i 3:18 Or "Simon the Zealot" or "Simon the Canaanean."

j 3:19 Iscariot is taken from an Aramaic derivative for "lock" (locksmith).

Jesus and the Ruler of Demons

20Then Jesus went home,ᵃ but once again a large crowd gathered around him, which prevented him from even eating a meal. 21When his own family heard that he was there, they went out to seize him, for they said, "He's insane!"

22The religious scholars who arrived from Jerusalem were saying, "Satanᵇ has possessed him! He casts out demons by the authority of the prince of demons!" 23Jesus called them to himself and spoke to them using parables. **"How can Satan cast out Satan? 24No kingdom can endure if it is divided against itself, 25and a splintered household will not be able to stand, for it is divided. 26And if Satan fights against himself he will not endure, and his end has come."**

27Jesus said to them,ᶜ **"Listen. No one is able to break into a mighty man's house and steal his property unless he first overpowers the mighty man and ties him up.ᵈ Then his entire house can be plundered and his possessions taken. 28I tell you this timeless truth: All sin can be forgiven, even all the blasphemies they speak. 29But there can never be forgiveness for the one who blasphemes against the Holy Spirit, for he is guilty of an eternal sin!"ᵉ** 30(This is because they said he was empowered by a demon spirit.)

---

a 3:20 This was likely the house of Peter the Rock and Andrew mentioned in Mark 1:29.

b 3:22 Or "Beelzelbul," another name for Satan, the ruler of demons.

c 3:27 This information is given in verse 30 and is positioned here for the sake of clarity of the English narrative.

d 3:27 Luke adds a phrase here: "The stronger one (Jesus) overpowers him." The stronger one is Jesus, who first defeated Satan in the wilderness ordeal and then destroyed him by the cross and resurrection (Hebrews 2:14). Bruising his head, Jesus now has Satan under his feet and will soon consign him to the lake of fire.

e 3:29 The information found in verse 30 is included in verse 27 for the sake of the English narrative.

Members of Jesus' True Family

³¹Then Jesus' mother and his brothers came and stood outside and sent a message to him, asking that he come out and speak with them.ᵃ ³²When the crowd sitting around Jesus heard this, they spoke up, and said to him, "Jesus, your mother and brothersᵇ are outside looking for you."

³³He answered them saying, **"Who is my true mother and my true brothers?"** ³⁴Then looking in the eyes of those who were sitting in a circle around him, he said, **"Here are my true family members.** ³⁵**For whoever does the will of God is my brother, my sister, and my mother!"**

---

a 3:31 It is likely that Jesus' family did not follow him, because they feared rejection by their community. This happened in Nazareth, after Jesus publicly stated that he was the fulfillment of Isaiah's prophecy of the Messiah and the townspeople wanted to kill Jesus by throwing him off a cliff. See Luke 4:18–29.

b 3:32 Some manuscripts include the words "and sisters."

Four

___

Parable of the Farmer Scattering Seed

¹Once again Jesus went to teach the people on the shore of Lake Galilee[a] and a massive crowd surrounded him. The crowd was so huge that he had to get into a boat and teach the people from there. ²He taught them many things by using parables[b] to illustrate spiritual truths, saying:

³"Consider this: A farmer went out to sow seeds. ⁴As he cast his seeds some of it fell along the beaten path and soon the birds came and ate it. ⁵Other seeds fell onto gravel with no topsoil and the seeds quickly sprouted since the soil had no depth. ⁶But when the days grew hot, the sprouts were scorched and withered because they had insufficient roots. ⁷Other seeds fell among the thorns, so when the seeds sprouted so did the thorns, crowding out the

___

a 4:1 Commonly known as the Sea of Galilee. It is interesting that Jesus left the house to go to the sea. The "house" suggests the "house of Israel," and the "sea" speaks of the non-Jewish peoples (i.e., the "sea of humanity").

b 4:2 The Aramaic and Greek use a word for "parable" that means "a metaphor, allegory, simile, illustration, comparison, figure of speech, riddle, or enigmatic saying that is meant to stimulate intense thought." Throughout Hebrew history, wise men, prophets, and teachers used parables and allegories as a preferred method of teaching spiritual truths. Poets would write their riddles and musicians would sing their proverbs with verbal imagery. Jesus never taught the people without using allegory and parables (Matthew 13:34 and Mark 4:34). As a true prophet, Jesus' preferred method of teaching was allegory. To deny the validity of allegorical teaching is to ignore the teaching methods of Jesus, the Living Word.

young plants so that they could produce no grain. [8]But some of the seeds fell onto good, rich soil that kept producing a good harvest. Some yielded thirty, some sixty—and some even one hundred times as much as was planted! [9]If you understand this, then you need to respond."[a]

The Purpose of Parables

[10]Afterwards, Jesus, his disciples and those close to him remained behind to ask Jesus about his parables. [11]He said to them, **"The privilege of intimately knowing the mystery of God's kingdom realm has been granted to you, but not to the others, where everything is revealed in parables.**[b]

> [12]**"For even when they see what I do, they will not understand, and when they, hear what I say, they will learn nothing, otherwise they would repent and be forgiven."**[c]

[13]Then he said to them, **"If you don't understand this parable, how will you understand any parable? [14]Let me explain: The farmer sows the Word as seed, [15]and what falls on the beaten path represents those who hear the Word, but immediately Satan appears and snatches it from their hearts. [16]The seed sown on gravel**

---

a 4:9 Or "The one with ears to hear should use them." We usually apply portions of this parable to unbelievers, but Jesus instructs us to apply it to ourselves. The four kinds of soils speak of four kinds of hearts: hard hearts, hollow hearts, half hearts, and whole hearts. With the first soil we see the activity of Satan, the second, that of the flesh, and the third, that of the world. Bearing fruit is never a problem with the seed but with the soil it falls upon.

b 4:11 Or "to the outsiders." The Aramaic is "backward ones." Jesus spoke allegorically so that those who didn't care to understand couldn't understand. Yet he knew that the hungry ones would seek out the hidden meaning of the parables and understand the secrets of God's kingdom realm. It is still that way today. See Proverbs 25:2.

c 4:12 See Isaiah 6:9–10.

represents those who hear the word and receive it joyfully, [17]but because their hearts fail to sink a deep root into the Word, they don't endure for long. For when trouble or persecution comes on account of the Word, they immediately wilt and fall away. [18]And the seed sown among thorns represents those who hear the Word, [19]but they allow the cares of this life and the seduction of wealth and the desires for other things to crowd out and choke the Word so that it produces nothing.

[20]"But the seed sown on good soil represents those who open their hearts to receive the Word and their lives bear good fruit— some yield a harvest of thirty, sixty, even one hundred times more than was sown!"

Parable of the Lamp

[21]He also gave them this parable: "No one lights a lamp[a] only to place it under a basket or under the bed. It is meant to be placed on a lampstand. [22]For there is nothing that is hidden that won't be disclosed, and there is no secret that won't be brought out into the light! [23]If you understand what I'm saying, you need to respond!"[b]

[24]Then he said to them, "Be diligent to understand the meaning behind everything you hear, for as you do, more understanding will be given to you. And according to the depth of your longing

---

a 4:21 The Jewish people considered the Torah, God's Word, to be a lamp that gives light to see and understand. Israel was meant to be a light that gives illumination to the nations. Jesus also calls his followers "the light of the world." See Matthew 5:14.

b 4:23 Or "The one with ears to hear should use them." The Aramaic is "If one brings a hearing ear for himself, he will hear."

to understand,[a] much more will be added to you. [25]For those who listen with open hearts will receive more revelation. But those who don't listen with open hearts will lose what little they think they have!"[b]

Parable of the Growing Seed

[26]Jesus also told them this parable: "God's kingdom realm is like someone spreading seed on the ground. [27]He goes to bed and gets up, day after day, and the seed sprouts and grows tall, though he knows not how. [28]All by itself it sprouts, and the soil produces a crop; first the green stem, then the head on the stalk, and then the fully developed grain in the head. [29]Then, when the grain is ripe, he immediately puts the sickle to the grain, because harvest time has come."[c]

Parable of the Tiny Mustard Seed

[30]And he told them this parable: "How can I describe God's kingdom realm? Let me illustrate it with this parable. [31]It is like the mustard seed, the tiniest of all the seeds, [32]yet when it springs up and grows, it becomes the largest plant in the garden. And with

---

a 4:24 Or "By the measure with which you measure, it will be measured to you." Some interpret this to refer to our relationships; i.e., "The way you treat others will be the way you will be treated." However, the context is clearly about having an open heart to receive and live in truth, and not hide it or have a closed heart to understand.

b 4:25 This verse contains a complicated ellipsis, which is a literary function of omitting certain information to invite discovery. The ellipsis of the text has been supplied by making explicit what is implicit in the context. The verse reads literally, "More will be given to the person who has (something), but a person who doesn't have (something), even what (something) they do have will be taken from him." The translation fills the ellipsis with the theme of the context—having an open heart to receive the truth of God. The parables of the sower and of the lamp are similar in that they speak of the heart that receives truth. The Word is a "seed" that grows within us and a "lamp" that glows within us.

c 4:29 This parable is only found in Mark's gospel. It teaches us that the reality of God's kingdom realm is like seed sown into the world that will grow through stages of maturity until the harvest.

so many enormous spreading branches, even birds can nest in its shade."[a]

Jesus Always Taught Using Parables

[33]Jesus used many parables such as these as he taught the people, and they learned according to their ability to understand. [34]He never spoke to them without using parables, but would wait until they were alone before he explained their meanings to his disciples.[b]

Jesus Stills a Storm

[35]Later that day, after it grew dark, Jesus said to his disciples, **"Let's cross over to the other side of the lake."** [36]After they had sent the crowd away, they shoved off from shore with him, as he had been teaching from the boat,[c] and there were other boats that sailed with them. [37]Suddenly, as they were crossing the lake, a ferocious tempest arose, with violent winds and waves that were crashing into the boat until it was all but swamped.[d] [38]But Jesus was calmly sleeping in the stern, resting on a cushion. [39]So they shook him awake, saying, "Teacher, don't you even care that we are all about to die!" Fully awake, he rebuked the storm and shouted to the sea, **"Hush! Calm**

---

a 4:32 Like the preceding parable, this is an allegorical way of describing the growth of God's kingdom realm. It may appear in the beginning as small and insignificant, yet it will grow until it becomes the greatest kingdom of all. Both of these parables teach us that God's kingdom is growing on the earth and not diminishing. See Ezekiel 17:22–24.

b 4:34 Jesus still delights to mystify those who follow him, but he waits until we are alone with him, and then he reveals the wonders of his grace and truth to our hearts.

c 4:36 The somewhat awkward construction of the Greek sentence "They took him along just as he was, in the boat" implies that Jesus was already in the boat where he had been sitting and teaching.

d 4:37 This gale of wind and ferocious tempest was demonic in nature, as Jesus was about to confront a powerful principality on the other side of the lake. (See Mark 5:1–20.) Jesus would not have rebuked the storm if it was from God. The Devil knew that if Jesus crossed to the other side, he would cast out the demon horde that had long terrorized the entire region.

down!" All at once the wind stopped howling and the water became perfectly calm.

⁴⁰Then he turned to his disciples and said to them, **"Why are you so afraid? Haven't you learned to trust yet?"** ⁴¹But they were overwhelmed with fear and awe and said to one another, "Who is this man who has such authority that even the wind and waves obey him?"

Five

A Demonized Man Set Free

¹They arrived at the other side of the lake, at the region of the Gerasenes.ᵃ ²As Jesus stepped ashore, a demon-possessed madman came out of the graveyard and confronted him. ³The man had been living there among the tombs of the dead, and no one was able to restrain him, not even with chains. ⁴For every time they attempted to chain his hands and feet with shackles, he would snap the chains and break the shackles in pieces. He was so strong that no one had the power to subdue him. Day and night he could be found lurking in the cemetery or in the vicinity, shrieking and mangling himself with stones!

⁶When he saw Jesus from a distance, he ran to him and threw himself down before him, ⁷screaming out at the top of his lungs, "Leave me alone, Jesus, Son of the Most High God! Swear in God's name that you won't torture me!" ⁸(For Jesus had already said to him, **"Come out of that man, you demon spirit!"**)

⁹Jesus said to him, **"What is your name?"**

---

a 5:1 This was a region of non-Jewish people who were raising swine, which was considered unclean by Jewish dietary laws. Gerasenes (or Gadarenes) were people who lived in a region opposite Galilee, on the southeastern side of the Lake of Galilee. See Matthew 8:28–34.

"Mob,"[a] he answered. "They call me Mob because there are thousands of us in his body!" [10]He begged Jesus repeatedly not to expel them out of the region.

[11]Nearby there was a large herd of pigs feeding on the hillside. [12]The demons begged him, "Send us into the pigs. Let us enter them!"

[13]So Jesus gave them permission, and the demon horde immediately came out of the man and went into the pigs! This caused the herd to rush madly down the steep slope and fall into the lake, drowning about two thousand pigs![b]

[14]Now, the herdsmen fled to the nearby villages, telling everyone what they saw as they ran through the countryside, and everyone came out to see what had happened. [15]When they found Jesus, they saw the demonized man sitting there, properly clothed and in his right mind. Seeing what had happened to the man who had thousands of demons, the people were terrified. [16]Those who had witnessed *this miracle* reported the news to the people and included what had happened to the pigs.[17]Then they asked Jesus to leave their region.[c]

[18]And as Jesus began to get into the boat to depart, the man who had been set free from demons asked him, "Could I go with you?" [19]Jesus answered, **"No,"** but said to him, **"Go back to your home and to your family and tell them what the Lord has done for you. Tell them how he had mercy on you."**

---

a 5:9 Or "Legion" (a Roman military unit of more than six thousand men). Mark gives twelve accounts of Jesus defeating demon spirits. The demons always recognized Jesus as God's Son.

b 5:13 Depending on weight, the cost of two thousand live pigs today could be as much as $250,000. The economic cost to the community over the loss of this herd was significant.

c 5:17 The people preferred swine to the Son of God. There is no indication that Jesus ever went back to their land.

²⁰So the man left and went into the region of Jordan and parts of Syriaᵃ to tell everyone he met about what Jesus had done for him, and all the people marveled!

Two Miracles—Healing and Resurrection

²¹After Jesus returned from across the lake, a huge crowd of people quickly gathered around him on the shoreline. ²²Just then, a man saw that it was Jesus, so he pushed through the crowd and threw himself down at his feet. His name was Jairus,ᵇ a Jewish official who was in charge of the synagogue. ²³He pleaded with Jesus, saying over and over, "Please come with me! My little daughter is at the point of death, *and she's only twelve years old!*ᶜ Come and lay your hands on her and heal her and she will live!"

²⁴Jesus went with him, and the huge crowd followed, pressing in on him from all sides.

²⁵Now, in the crowd that day was a woman who had suffered horribly from continual bleeding for twelve years.ᵈ ²⁶She had endured a great deal under the care of various doctors, yet in spite of spending all she had on their treatments, she was not getting better, but worse. ²⁷When she heard about Jesus' *healing power,* she pushed

---

a 5:20 Or "Decapolis," which means "Ten Cities." The region of these ten cities was Jordan and parts of Syria, including Damascus. These cities were Greek and Roman cultural centers of that day. It is a wonder of grace that Jesus used a man who once had thousands of demons to bring God's truth to thousands of people. After he was set free, he became a missionary evangelist, telling others what Jesus Christ had done for him. No wonder the people marveled when they heard his story!

b 5:22 Jairus (taken from the Hebrew name Jair) means "he enlightens" or "he shines the light." Some have taken it to mean "Jehovah enlightens," but God's name is not found in the name Jairus.

c 5:23 This is taken from verse 42 and is brought in at this sequence of the narrative for the sake of clarity and in contrast with the woman who suffered for twelve years (verse 25).

d 5:25 The daughter of Jairus was twelve years old; this woman had suffered for twelve years. Jesus touched the girl; the woman touched Jesus. The two intertwining miracles in this chapter speak of Jesus healing the Gentiles (Mark identifies her as a Syro-Phoenecian Gentile) and raising Israel back to life (Jairus' Jewish daughter). On his way to raise the Jewish girl, he stopped to heal the Gentile woman. This is what is happening today with Jews and non-Jews.

through the crowd and came up from behind him and touched his prayer shawl.[a] [28]For she kept saying to herself, "If only I could touch his clothes, I know I will be healed."[b] [29]As soon as her hand touched him, her bleeding immediately stopped! She knew it, for she could feel her body instantly being healed of her disease!

[30]Jesus knew at once that someone had touched him, for he felt the power that always surged around him[c] had passed through him for someone to be healed. He turned and spoke to the crowd, saying, **"Who touched my clothes?"**[d]

[31]His disciples answered, "What do mean, who touched you? Look at this huge crowd—they're all pressing up against you." [32]But Jesus' eyes swept across the crowd, looking for the one who had touched him for healing.

[33]When the woman who experienced this miracle[e] realized what had happened to her, she came before him, trembling with fear, and threw herself down at his feet, *saying, "I was the one who touched you."* And she told him her story of what had just happened.

---

a 5:27 Or "cloak (outer garment)." As a Jewish man, Jesus would have had over his shoulders a prayer shawl (tallit). The blue tassel on the corner of the prayer shawl was said to symbolize all the commandments and promises of God. See Numbers 15:38–40. The Hebrew word for "fringe" or "border (of a garment)" can also mean "wing." Some have interpreted Malachi 4:2 ("healing in his wings") as a reference to the tassels of the prayer shawl.

b 5:28 The Greek word is *sozo* and has many possible meanings, including "safe and sound, healed, delivered, made whole, rescued, restored, and saved." This is what Jesus does for us today. See Hebrews 13:8.

c 5:30 This is a literal reading of a unique phrase in Greek construction. It could be translated "The power that keeps going out of him went out from him." There was a glorious power that kept going out around Jesus Christ, drawing others to him and healing those he touched, and in this case, healing a woman who touched him in faith. Jesus knew that the power of God was always emanating around him, yet it had flowed through him to someone in the crowd. This same miracle was repeated with Peter the Rock in Acts 5:15.

d 5:30 Jesus already knew the answer to his question. He wanted the woman to come forward and acknowledge her healing. There were crowds around Jesus, the living Word. Many today crowd around the written Word. But only those who "touch" the Scriptures in faith receive its promises, just like the sick woman who received her healing.

e 5:33 As translated from the Aramaic.

³⁴Then Jesus said to her, **"Daughter, because you dared to believe, your faith has healed you. Go with peace in your heart, and be free from your suffering!"**

³⁵And before he had finished speaking, people arrived from Jairus' house *and pushed through the crowd* to give Jairus the news: "There's no need to trouble the master any longer—your daughter has died." ³⁶But Jesus refused to listen to what they were told*ᵃ* and said to the Jewish official, **"Don't yield to fear. All you need to do is to keep on believing."** ³⁷*So they left for his home,* but Jesus didn't allow anyone to go with them except Peter and the two brothers, Jacob and John.

³⁸When they arrived at the home of the synagogue ruler, they encountered a noisy uproar among the people, for they were all weeping and wailing. ³⁹Upon entering the home, Jesus said to them, **"Why all this grief and weeping? Don't you know the girl is not dead but merely asleep?"** ⁴⁰Then everyone began to ridicule and made fun of him. But he threw*ᵇ* them all outside.

Then he took the child's father and mother and his three disciples and went into the room where the girl was lying. ⁴¹He tenderly clasped the child's hand in his and said to her in Aramaic, **"Talitha koum,"*ᶜ*** which means, "Little girl,*ᵈ* wake up from the sleep of death." ⁴²Instantly the twelve-year-old girl sat up, stood to her feet,

---

a 5:36 At times there must be a holy "deafness" to the words of others, words that would distract us from the purposes of God. See Isaiah 42:19–20.

b 5:40 The Greek word *ekballo* is often used for driving out demons. It implies a forceful action of authority.

c 5:41 One of the many references in the New Testament proving that the language of Jesus was Aramaic.

d 5:41 The Aramaic word *talitha* can also mean "little lamb." The Greek word used here is *korasion*, which may be a hypocorism, similar to "sweetheart." The tenderness of this moment is obvious in the text.

and started walking around the room! Everyone was overcome with astonishment in seeing this miracle! [43]Jesus had them bring her something to eat. And he repeatedly cautioned them that they were to tell no one about what had happened.[a]

a 5:43 There was nothing secretive about this resurrection miracle of the twelve-year-old girl. It would be hard to keep hidden from the people. Jesus was cautioning them because of the reaction of certain religious authorities who were convinced that Jesus was working wonders by the power of Satan. Later on, the miracle of Lazarus being raised from the dead was what triggered the arrest of Jesus.

Six

Jesus Rejected in Nazareth

¹Afterward, Jesus left Capernaum[a] and returned with his disciples to Nazareth, his hometown. ²On the Sabbath, he went to teach in the synagogue. Everyone who heard his teaching was overwhelmed with astonishment. They said among themselves, "What incredible wisdom has been given to him! Where did he receive such profound insights?[b] And what mighty miracles flow through his hands! ³Isn't this Miriam's son, the carpenter,[c] the brother of Jacob, Joseph,[d] Judah, and Simon? And don't his sisters all live here in Nazareth?" And they took offense at him.

⁴Jesus said to them, **"A prophet is treated with honor everywhere except in his own hometown, among his relatives, and in his own house."** ⁵He was unable to do any great miracle in Nazareth,[e]

---

a 6:1 The healing of the woman and the resurrection of Jairus' daughter were both done in Capernaum.

b 6:2 Or "Where did he get these things (insights, understanding, ideas, teachings)?"

c 6:3 The Greek word *tekton* can be translated "carpenter," "metal worker," "sculptor," "artisan," "stone worker," or "builder."

d 6:3 Or "Joses."

e 6:5 Nazareth was the only place recorded in the Gospels that Jesus was unable (because of their unbelief) to do miracles.

except to heal a few sick people by laying his hands upon them. [6]He was amazed at the depth of their unbelief![a]

Then Jesus went out into the different villages and taught the people.

Jesus Sends Out the Twelve Apostles

[7]Jesus gathered his twelve disciples and imparted to them his authority to cast out demons. Then he sent them out in pairs with these instructions: [8-9]**"Take only your staff and the sandals on your feet—no bread, no knapsack, no extra garment, and no money.[b] [10]And whatever house you enter, stay there until you leave the area. [11]Whatever community does not welcome you or receive your message, leave it behind. And as you go, shake the dust off your feet as a testimony against them."[c]**

[12]So they went out and preached publicly that everyone should repent. [13]They cast out many demons and anointed many sick people with oil and healed them.

Death of John the Immerser

[14]King Herod soon heard about Jesus, for the name of Jesus was on everyone's lips. Some were even saying about him, "John the Immerser has been raised from the dead, and that's why miraculous

a 6:6 This is one of two instances where Jesus was amazed. The other is found in Matthew 8:10. Both refer to the response of faith. Here it is the great unbelief of those who knew Jesus and lived in his hometown of Nazareth (Jews). The other is the great faith of the Roman military captain (a Gentile). We have no record of Jesus ever returning to Nazareth. He made Capernaum his base of ministry while in the province of Galilee.

b 6:8–9 Or "copper coins inside your belt."

c 6:11 The Aramaic and some Greek manuscripts add a sentence: "Truly, I tell you that it will be more tolerable for Sodom and Gomorrah in the day of judgment than for that city."

powers flow from him!" 15Others said, "No, he's Elijah!" While others said, "He's a prophet, like one of the prophets of old!"

16When Herod heard what the people were saying, he concluded, "I beheaded John, and now he's raised from the dead!" 17-18For Herod had John arrested and thrown into prison for repeatedly rebuking him in public, saying, "You have no right to marry Herodias, the wife of your brother Philip! You are violating the law of God!"[a]

19This infuriated Herodias, and she held a bitter grudge against him and wanted John executed. 20But Herod both feared and stood in awe[b] of John and kept him safely in custody, because he was convinced that he was a righteous and holy man. Every time Herod heard John speak, it disturbed his soul, but he was drawn to him and enjoyed listening to his words.

21But Herodias found her opportunity to have John killed—it was on the king's birthday! Herod prepared a great banquet and invited all his officials, military commanders, and the leaders of the province of Galilee to celebrate with him on his birthday. 22On the day of the feast, his stepdaughter, the daughter of Herodias,[c] came to honor the king with a beautiful dance, and she flattered him.[d] Her dancing greatly pleased the king and his guests, so he said to the girl, "You can ask me for anything you want and I will give it to you!" 23And he repeated it in front of everyone, with a vow to complete his promise to her: "Anything you desire and it will be yours! I'll even share my kingdom with you!"

---

a 6:17-18 See Leviticus 18:16 and 20:21.
b 6:20 The Greek text can also mean "deep respect" or that Herod "feared John."
c 6:22 Although unnamed, church history and tradition identifies her as Salome, not to be confused with the Salome who was a witness of the crucifixion (Mark 15:40).
d 6:22 Or "She fascinated him."

²⁴She immediately left the room and said to her mother, "What should I ask for?" Her mother answered, "The head of John the Immerser on a platter!" ²⁵So she hurried back to the king and made her request: "I want you to bring me the head of John the Immerser on a platter—and I want it right now!"

²⁶Deeply grieved, the king regretted[a] his promise to her, but since he had made his vow in front of all his honored guests, he couldn't deny her request. ²⁷So without delay the king ordered an executioner to bring John's head, and he went and beheaded John in prison. ²⁸He brought his head on a platter and gave it to the girl, and the girl brought it to her mother. ²⁹When John's followers heard what had happened, they came and removed his body and laid it in a tomb.

Jesus Multiplies Food to Feed Five Thousand

³⁰The apostles *returned from their mission*[b] and gathered around Jesus and told him everything they had done and taught.

³¹There was such a swirl of activity around Jesus, with so many people coming and going, that they were unable to even eat a meal. So Jesus said to his disciples, **"Come, let's take a break and find a secluded place where you can rest a while."** ³²They slipped away and left by sailboat for a deserted spot. ³³But many of the people saw them leaving and realized where they were headed, so they took off running along the shore. Then people from the surrounding towns joined them in the chase, and a large crowd got there ahead of them.

---

a 6:26 The Aramaic is "The king was tied in a knot."

b 6:30 Jesus had sent the apostles into the Galilean villages to preach and cast out demons (6:7-13), and they are now returning to report back to him.

34By the time Jesus came ashore, a massive crowd was waiting. At the sight of them, his heart was filled with compassion,[a] because they seemed like wandering sheep who had no shepherd.[b] So he taught them many things.

35Late that afternoon, his disciples said, "It's getting really late and we're here in this remote place with nothing to eat. 36You should send the crowds away so they can go into the surrounding villages and buy food for themselves."

37But he answered them, **"You give them something to eat."**

"Are you sure?" they replied. "You really want us to go buy them supper? It would cost a small fortune[c] to feed all these thousands of hungry people."

38**"How many loaves of bread do you have?"** he asked. **"Go and see."** After they had looked around, they came back and said, "Five—plus a couple of fish."

39Then he instructed them to organize the crowd and have them sit down in groups on the grass. 40So they had them sit down in groups[d] of hundreds and fifties. 41Then Jesus took the five loaves and two fish, gazed into heaven, and gave thanks to God. He broke the bread and the two fish and distributed them to his disciples to serve the people—*and the food was multiplied in front of their eyes!* 42Everyone had plenty to eat and was fully satisfied. 43Then the

---

a 6:34 The Aramaic is "nurturing love toward them."

b 6:34 See Numbers 27:17 and Ezekiel 34:5.

c 6:37 Or "two hundred denarii (silver coins)." A denarius was the going rate for a day's wage. This would equal nearly eight months' wages.

d 6:40 There are two Greek words used for groups in this context. In verse 39 it is the Greek word *symposion*, which is used most frequently for drinking parties (rows of guests). The word *prasai* found in verse 40 can also mean "garden plots" or "flower beds." Spread out over the hillside the people would have looked like flower beds, planted in green pastures, drinking in the miracle power of Jesus. See Psalm 23:2.

twelve disciples picked up what remained, and each of them ended up with a basket full of leftovers! [44]All together, five thousand families were fed that day![a]

Jesus Walks on Water

[45]After everyone had their meal, Jesus instructed his disciples to get back into the boat and go on ahead of him and sail to the other side to Bethsaida.[b] [46]So he dispersed the crowd, said good-bye to his disciples, then slipped away to pray on the mountain.

[47]As night fell, the boat was in the middle of the lake and Jesus was alone on land. [48]The wind was against the disciples and he could see[c] that they were straining at the oars, trying to make headway.

When it was almost morning,[d] Jesus came to them, walking on the surface of the water, and he started to pass by them.[e] [49-50]When they all saw him walking on the waves, they thought he was a ghost and screamed out in terror. But he said to them at once, **"Don't yield to fear. Have courage. It's really me—I Am!"**[f]

[51]Then he came closer and climbed into the boat with them, and immediately the stormy wind became still. They were completely and utterly overwhelmed with astonishment [52]because they failed to

---

a 6:44 Or "five thousand men." There were women and children present as well, but it would have not been common for women and children to come by themselves. These five thousand men represented their households. This miracle is the only miracle recorded in all four gospels.

b 6:45 This is Beit-Tside, which in Aramaic and Hebrew is "the fishing place."

c 6:48 Seeing them from land in the dark was an obvious miracle, for evening had come and Jesus was a great distance from them while they were in the middle of the lake. Jesus sees and knows the struggles each of us go through.

d 6:48 Or "about the fourth watch of the night."

e 6:48 To pass by them is somewhat similar to God "passing by Moses" when he was on Sinai. See Exodus 33:19 and 22.

f 6:49–50 In both Greek and Aramaic, this reads, "I AM (the Living God)," an obvious statement that Jesus is "the great I Am" and there is nothing to be afraid of. This is the same statement God made to Moses in front of the burning bush. See also Matthew 14:27 and John 8:58.

learn the lesson of the *miracle*[a] *of* the loaves, and their hearts were unwilling to learn the lesson.[b]

Jesus the Healer

[53]They made landfall at Gennesaret and anchored there.[c] [54]The moment they got out of the boat, everyone recognized that it was Jesus, *the healer!* [55]So they ran throughout the region, telling the people, "Bring all the sick—even those too sick to walk and bring them on mats!" [56]Wherever he went, in the countryside, villages, or towns, they placed the sick on mats in the streets or in public places[d] and begged him, saying, "Just let us touch the tassel of your prayer shawl!"[e] And all who touched him were instantly healed!

---

a 6:52 Or "They didn't understand about the loaves." That is, they didn't understand the lesson that the miracle was meant to teach them—that God has the power to deliver us, no matter what the limitation. Also, the miracle was that the bread multiplied in their hands, so they likewise had the power to rebuke the stormy wind and sail through to the other side, even if Jesus were to pass them. He wanted them to see things in a new light and know the authority that they now carried. The two lessons of the multiplied loaves were 1) that Jesus had all power to meet every need, and 2) that the disciples carried this power with them, for the bread multiplied in their hands. They were also a part of the miracle. See also Mark 8:14–21. The two great miracles of Israel were also duplicated here. The "crossing of the sea" and the "bread (manna)" that fell from heaven.

b 6:52 Or "Their minds were dull" or "unwilling to learn," or "Their hearts had been hardened." The implication is that they were unwilling to accept new information. Every miracle carries a message.

c 6:53 Apparently, they were blown off course, since they were headed for Bethsaida. Gennesaret is a plain not far from Capernaum on the northwest side of the lake.

d 6:56 Or "marketplace."

e 6:56 The blue tassel on the corner of the prayer shawl was said to symbolize all the commandments and promises of God. See Numbers 15:38–40. The Hebrew word for "fringe" or "border (of a garment)" can also mean "wing." Some have interpreted Malachi 4:2 ("healing in his wings") as a reference to the tassels of the prayer shawl.

Seven

Jesus Breaks Religious Traditions

¹One day, those known as the Pharisees and certain religious scholars came from Jerusalem and gathered around Jesus. ²They were shocked[a] to find that some of Jesus' disciples ate bread without first observing the prescribed Jewish ritual of hand washing before eating their meal. ³(For the Pharisees, like all other Jews, will not eat without first performing a ritual of pouring water over their cupped hands[b] to keep the tradition of the elders. ⁴Similarly, when returning from the marketplace, they ceremonially wash themselves[c] before eating. They also observed many other traditions, such as ceremonially washing cups, pitchers, and kettles.)[d]

⁵So the Pharisees and religious scholars asked Jesus, "Why don't your disciples live according to the age-old traditions passed

---

a 7:2 As translated from the Aramaic.

b 7:3 Or "with a fist." Some have surmised this was a thorough washing from the hand to the elbow. But it was most likely water poured over cupped hands. This is not taught in the Torah, but was insisted on because of the tradition of the elders. A few Greek manuscripts and the Aramaic read, "They do not eat unless they wash their hands carefully," with no mention of a fist.

c 7:4 The Aramaic is "If they do not bathe, they do not eat."

d 7:4 Some manuscripts add "dining couches." Some Aramaic manuscripts add "beds (mats)." This ceremonial sprinkling amounted to nothing more than religious rules and customs, but none of them were commanded in the writings of Moses—they were the traditions of men.

down by our elders? They should first ceremonially wash their hands before eating."

⁶Jesus replied, "You are frauds and hypocrites! How accurately[a] did Isaiah prophesy about you phonies when he said:

'These people honor me with their words
    while their hearts run far away from me!
⁷Their worship is nothing more than a charade!
    For they continue to insist
    that their man-made traditions
    are equal to the instructions of God.'[b]

⁸"You abandon God's commandments just to keep men's rituals, such as ceremonially washing utensils, cups, and other things."[c]

⁹Then he added, "How skillful you've become in rejecting God's law in order to maintain your man-made set of rules. ¹⁰For example, Moses taught us:

'Honor your father and your mother,'[d]

and,

'Whoever insults or mistreats his father or mother
    must be put to death.'[e]

¹¹"But your made-up rules allow a person to say to his parents, 'I've decided to take the support you were counting on from me

---

a 7:6 Or "excellently."
b 7:7 See Isaiah 29:13 LXX.
c 7:8 Some manuscripts omit the last clause. It is found in the Aramaic and the majority of Greek texts.
d 7:10 See Exodus 20:12 and Deuteronomy 5:16.
e 7:10 See Exodus 21:17 and Leviticus 20:9.

and make it my holy offering to God, and that will be your blessing instead.'[a] [12]How convenient! The rules you teach exempt him from providing for his aged parents. [13]Do you really think God will honor your traditions passed down to others, making up these rules that nullify God's Word? And you're doing many other things like that."

Jesus Explains What Truly Defiles

[14]Then Jesus called the crowd together again, saying, "Hear my words, all of you, and take them to heart. [15]What truly contaminates a person is not what he puts into his body, but what comes out. That's what makes a person defiled."[b]

[17]When Jesus went back home and away from the crowd, his disciples *acknowledged that they didn't understand the meaning of the parable and* asked him to explain it. [18]He answered them, "Are you as dull as the rest? Don't you understand that you are not defiled by what you eat? [19]For the food you swallow doesn't enter your heart, but goes into your stomach, only to pass out into the sewer." (This means all foods are clean.)[c] [20]He added, "Words and deeds pollute a person, not food. [21]Evil originates from inside a person. Coming out of a human heart are evil schemes,[d] sexual immorality,[e] theft, murder, [22]adultery, greed, wickedness,

---

a 7:11 As translated from the Aramaic. The Greek is "Whatever you would have gained from me will be *corban* (an offering)." *Corban* (*qorban*) is an Aramaic word that implies that a person is pure, sincere, and pious when he makes an offering to God. In this case, people would simply speak the word *corban* over the money they were obligated to use in support of their aged parents, and that would exempt them from their duty to give it. Jesus disapproved of this practice, as it nullified God's commands. Words themselves don't count with God; he seeks justice and obedience from the heart.

b 7:15 Some Greek manuscripts and the Aramaic add verse 16, "If anyone has ears to hear, let him hear."

c 7:19 The words in parenthesis are added by the author (Mark).

d 7:21 Or "depraved thoughts."

e 7:21 This is the Greek word *porneía* (the root word from which we get *pornography*). The literal meaning is "to sell off oneself (into sexual impurity)."

treachery, debauchery,[a] jealousy,[b] slander,[c] arrogance,[d] and recklessness.[e] 23All these corrupt things emerge from within and constantly pollute a person."

Jesus and a Foreign Woman

24Jesus set out from there to go into the non-Jewish region of Tyre.[f] He intended to slip into a house unnoticed, but people found out that he was there. 25But when a woman whose daughter had a demon spirit heard he was there, she came and threw herself down at his feet. 26She was not Jewish, but a foreigner,[g] born in the part of Syria known as Phoenicia.[h] She begged him repeatedly to cast the demon out of her daughter. 27Finally he said to her, **"First let my children be fed and satisfied, for it isn't fair to take the children's bread[i] and throw it to the little dogs."**[j]

---

a 7:22 Or "indecency."

b 7:22 Or "an evil eye," which is an Aramaic idiom for stinginess.

c 7:22 The Aramaic is "blasphemy."

d 7:22 The Aramaic is "boasting."

e 7:22 Or "senselessness."

f 7:24 Or "the region of Tyre and Sidon." (Some manuscripts do not have Sidon.) These two cities are located in Lebanon on the Mediterranean coast.

g 7:26 Or "Greek." The Jews considered the word Greek to mean anyone who was not a Jew, not necessarily a person of Greek descent.

h 7:26 This story, in light of the culture of that time, is phenomenal. She was a foreign-born woman with a demonized daughter. Combined, these characteristics made her an unlikely candidate to seek out a Jewish healer. The racial divide of that day was quite pronounced, but love and faith overcome every barrier, including racial prejudice. In Matthew 15:22, the Hebrew Matthew text describes her as "a Canaanite merchant woman." Canaan included the region of modern-day Lebanon and parts of Syria. A Canaanite would refer to a non-Jewish person who lived in that region. In this region, Jezebel established Baal worship and there her body was eventually thrown to the dogs. Here Jesus heals a woman and brings her into the true worship of God.

i 7:27 "Children" is a metaphor for the Jewish people (children of Israel), and the "children's bread" becomes a metaphor for healing or casting out demons.

j 7:27 Or "little pet dogs." The term translated "dog" here is the diminutive form of the Greek kuon. Calling her a household pet was not meant as an ethnic slur, but was used to describe an impure (unclean) mind. See Matthew 7:6, Philippians 3:2, 2 Peter 2:22, and Revelation 22:15. Using the metaphors of children, children's bread, and dogs was the way Jesus tested her faith and revealed her strong confidence in Jesus' power to heal her daughter. She saw Jesus as "Lord" and received her miracle.

²⁸She answered, "How true that is, Lord. But even puppies under the family table are allowed to eat the little children's crumbs."

²⁹Then Jesus said to her, **"That's a good reply! Now, because you said this, you may go. The demon has permanently left your daughter."** ³⁰And when she returned home, she found her daughter resting quietly on the couch, completely set free from the demon!

Jesus Heals a Deaf Man

³¹After this, Jesus left the coastland of Tyre and came through Sidon on his way to the Lake of Galilee and over into regions of Syria.ᵃ ³²Some people brought to him a deaf man with a severe speech impediment. They pleaded with Jesus to place his hands on him and heal him.

³³So Jesus led him away from the crowd to a private spot. Then he stuck his fingers into the man's ears and placed some of his saliva on the man's tongue.ᵇ ³⁴Then he gazed into heaven,ᶜ sighed deeply, and spoke to the man's ears and tongue, **"Ethpathakh,"** which is Aramaicᵈ for "Open up, now!"ᵉ

³⁵At once the man's ears opened and he could hear perfectly, and his tongue was untied and he began to speak normally. ³⁶Jesus ordered everyone to keep this miracle a secret, but the more he told

---

a 7:31 Or "the Decapolis," which means "Ten Cities," all of which were located in Syria. (See Mark 5:20 and accompanying footnote.) Jesus headed southeast to the lake of Galilee. This trek was many miles and would have taken him days to arrive.

b 7:33 The saliva of firstborn sons in the Jewish culture of Jesus' time was considered to have power to heal infirmities.

c 7:34 The Aramaic is "Then he focused on (or contemplated) heaven."

d 7:34 Aramaic was the language of Jesus and his disciples and continues to be spoken today. The spelling of *Ethpathakh* has been adjusted to fit proper Aramaic instead of the transliterated Greek text, which is unintelligible, possibly due to a scribal error.

e 7:34 The phrase "open up" is the same wording used in the Hebrew of Isaiah 61:1, "Open the prison doors." It furthermore refers to the opening of the eyes of the blind and the ears of the deaf.

them not to, the more the news spread! [37]The people were absolutely beside themselves and astonished beyond measure.[a] And they began to declare, "Everything he does is wonderful![b] He even makes the deaf hear and the mute speak!"

---

a 7:37 The Greek text uses an unusual construction, found nowhere else in the New Testament, to describe the utter astonishment of the people over this miracle. Mark alone records the two miracles of healing found in this chapter. One was a deaf man, the other a blind man. Jesus led them both away from the unbelief of others to work his miracle and healed them with his saliva. (Later, wicked men would spit upon him.) In both cases, Jesus told the men he healed not to tell others, but they did. He tells us to spread the good news, and we don't.

b 7:37 Or "beautiful," "perfect," "admirable," or "marvelous." This verse can also be translated "He has made everything beautiful" or "He has made everything ideally."

Eight

Jesus Multiplies Food Again

¹During those days, another massive crowd gathered to hear Jesus, and again, there was no food and the people were hungry. So Jesus called his disciples to come near him and said to them, ²**"My heart goes out to this crowd, for they've already been here with me for three days with nothing to eat. ³I'm concerned that if I send them home hungry, they'll be exhausted along the way, for some of them have come a long, long way just to be with me."**

⁴His disciples replied, "But could anyone possibly get enough food to satisfy a crowd this size out here in this isolated place?"

⁵He asked them, **"How many loaves of flatbread have you got?"**

"Seven," they replied.

⁶Jesus instructed the crowd to sit down on the grass. After he took the seven loaves, he gave thanks to God, broke them, and started handing them to his disciples. They kept distributing the bread until they had served the entire crowd.

⁷They also had a few small fish, and after giving thanks for these, Jesus had his disciples serve them to the crowd. ⁸Everyone ate until they were satisfied. Then the disciples gathered up the broken

pieces and filled seven large baskets[a] with the leftovers. [9]About four thousand[b] people ate the food that had been multiplied! Then he dismissed the crowd.[c]

[10]Afterward, Jesus got into a boat and sailed to the vicinity of Dalmanutha.[d]

The Pharisees Demand a Sign

[11]As soon as Jesus landed,[e] he was confronted by the Pharisees,[f] who argued with Jesus and tested him. They demanded that he give them a miraculous sign from heaven.

[12]And with a deep sigh from his spirit, he said, **"What drives this generation to clamor for a sign? Listen to the truth: there will absolutely be no sign given to this generation!"**[g] [13]Then he turned and left them, got back into the boat, and crossed over to the opposite shore.

---

a 8:8 This is the same word used for Paul escaping from Damascus by being lowered down the city wall in a basket (hamper). These baskets were large enough for a man to hide in. See Acts 9:25.

b 8:9 Although only four thousand people are mention by Mark, it is possible that there were four thousand men, not including women and children. See Matthew 15:32–39 and 2 Kings 4:42–44. All four gospels record the feeding of the five thousand, but only Matthew and Mark give us the feeding of the four thousand. Many have called this the forgotten miracle. Jesus multiplied food twice with miracle power. Because of the locations of these two miracles, it is believed that the five thousand were mostly Jews and the four thousand mentioned here were mostly Gentiles. First the Jew, then the Gentile. First there were twelve baskets of leftovers, then seven large baskets full. Twelve is a distinctively Jewish number representing government, and seven represents fullness, indicating the fullness of blessing going out to entire world. The Bread of Life, Jesus Christ, is now our feast.

c 8:9 The Aramaic uses an idiomatic saying that can mean "Jesus ended their fast."

d 8:10 Some scholars believe that this may have been near Magdala on the western shore of Lake Galilee. See Matthew 15:39. The Aramaic word for Dalmanutha means "the land of oppression."

e 8:11 Or "immediately."

f 8:11 Or "separated ones" who saw themselves as Jewish purists and guardians of religious orthodoxy. Although the text does not say what sign they were demanding, they were requiring proof of Jesus' divine mission and ministry. The text does imply that they were disingenuous and wanted only to discredit Jesus.

g 8:12 The Greek word for "generation" can also mean "a tribe or nation."

Jesus Warns of the Yeast of the Pharisees and of Herod

[14]Now, the disciples had forgotten to take bread with them, except for one loaf of flatbread. [15]*And as they were sailing across the lake,* Jesus repeatedly warned them, **"Be on your guard against the yeast[a] inside of the Pharisees and the yeast inside of Herod!"** [16]But the disciples had no clue what Jesus was talking about, so they began to discuss it among themselves, saying, "Is he saying this because we forgot to bring bread?"

[17]Knowing what they were thinking, Jesus said to them, **"Why all this fussing over forgetting to bring bread? Do you still not see or understand what I say to you? Are your hearts still hard? [18]You have good eyes, yet you still don't see, and you have good ears, yet you still don't hear, neither do you remember. [19]When I multiplied the bread to feed more than five thousand people, how many baskets full of leftovers did you gather afterward?"**

"Twelve," they replied.

[20]**"And when I multiplied food to feed over four thousand, how many large baskets full of leftovers did you gather afterwards?"**

"Seven," they replied.

[21]**"Then how is it that you still don't get it?"**

Jesus Heals Blind Eyes

[22]When they arrived at Bethsaida, some people brought a blind man to Jesus, begging him to touch him and heal him. [23]So Jesus led him, as his sighted guide, outside the village. He placed his saliva on the

---

a 8:15 The yeast Jesus is referring to here is hypocrisy. See Luke 12:1. The yeast of religious and political hypocrisy is what Jesus warned them to avoid.

man's eyes[a] and covered them with his hands.[b] Then he asked him, **"Now do you see anything?"**

24"Yes," he said. "My sight is coming back! I'm beginning to see people, but they look like trees—walking trees."

25Jesus put his hands over the man's eyes a second time and made him look up. The man opened his eyes wide and he could see everything perfectly. His eyesight was completely restored! 26Then Jesus sent him home with these instructions: **"Go home, but don't tell anyone what happened, not even the people of your own village."**[c]

Peter the Rock Receives Revelation from God

27Then Jesus and his disciples walked[d] to the villages near Caesarea Philippi.[e] On the way, he posed this question to his disciples: **"Who do the people say that I am?"**

28They replied, "Some say John the Immerser, others say Elijah[f] the prophet, and still others say you must be one of the prophets."

29He asked them, **"But who do you say that I am?"**

---

a 8:23 This is not the common word for "eyes." The Greek word *omma* can refer to both physical and spiritual sight. See also Matthew 20:34.

b 8:23 The Aramaic can be translated "Jesus placed his hands over his eyes and brought light."

c 8:26 As translated from the Aramaic and some Greek manuscripts. The Greek contains many variations of this statement. Other manuscripts read, "Go to your house, and if you go into the village, don't tell anyone what happened." Others read, "Do not even go into the village."

d 8:27 This would likely have been a two-day journey of thirty miles north from Bethsaida.

e 8:27 This was a beautiful area north of the Lake of Galilee near Tel-Dan. Located at the foothills of Mount Hermon, it was an ancient Roman city rebuilt by Herod Philip in honor of Tiberius Caesar.

f 8:28 For the Jews, the return of Elijah would signal the end of days. See Malachi 4:5.

Peter[a] the Rock spoke up, saying, "You are the Messiah,[b] the Son of the Living God!"[c]

30Then he warned them not to breathe a word of this to anyone.

Jesus Prophesies His Death and Resurrection

31From then on, Jesus began to tell his disciples that he, the Son of Man, was destined to go to Jerusalem and suffer great injustice[d] from the elders, leading priests, and religious scholars. He also explained that he would be killed and three days later be raised to life again. 32Jesus opened his heart and spoke freely with his disciples, explaining all these things to them.[e]

Then Peter the Rock took him aside and rebuked him.[f] 33But Jesus turned around, and glancing at all of the other disciples,[g] he rebuked Peter, saying, **"Get out of my sight, Satan!**[h] **For your heart is not set on God's plan but man's!"**[i]

---

a 8:29 The Aramaic is "Shimon (Simeon)," which presents an interesting word play. *Shimon* means "he who hears." Simon Peter heard the question posed by Jesus and answered it. But he also heard the revelation from the Father that Jesus is the Messiah, God's Son. See Matthew 16:17. Simon is the first one of the disciples who truly heard the Father's revelation of the identity of Jesus Christ.

b 8:29 Or "the Christ," which means "the Anointed One (Messiah)."

c 8:29 As translated from the Aramaic and a small number of Greek manuscripts.

d 8:31 This great injustice refers to the beatings, mockings, rejection, and illegal trial Jesus endured. To have the Messiah suffer was contrary to every belief system among the Jews. The Messiah was to be the King of Israel, surrounded with glory, not suffering. Mark gives us three instances of Jesus prophesying of his death and resurrection (8:31, 9:31, and 10:33). Each time Jesus made this prediction, the disciples were confused and unable to understand. So Jesus took the opportunity to explain what being his follower really entailed (8:34–38, 9:33–37, and 10:35–45).

e 8:32 Or "He spoke openly (boldly, plainly, freely, honestly) about this."

f 8:32 Although Mark does not state what Peter was saying to Jesus, he was likely rebuking him for not understanding the role of the Messiah-King, who was going to suffer and die, but who would rise to power and bring glory to Israel. Peter wanted Jesus to come up with another plan. Yet Peter was the who was mistaken, not Jesus. How many times have we assumed we had a better plan for our lives than God had? One moment Peter speaks profoundly about Jesus' identity, and the next he rebukes the Messiah for choosing the wrong path.

g 8:33 Jesus knew that Peter was merely being the spokesman for all twelve disciples, voicing their opinion to Jesus on their behalf.

h 8:33 Peter's rebuke of Jesus became, as it were, the words of Satan himself. The word used for Satan here means "adversary."

i 8:33 The Aramaic can be translated "For you never cheer God but the children of men!"

What It Means to Be a Follower of Jesus

³⁴Jesus summoned the crowd, along with his disciples, and had them gather around. And he said to them: **"If you truly want to follow me, you should at once completely disown your own life. And you must be willing to share my cross and experience it as your own, as you continually surrender to my ways.**ᵃ ³⁵**For if you let your life go for my sake and for the sake of the gospel, you will continually experience true life.**ᵇ **But if you choose to keep your life for yourself, you will forfeit what you try to keep.** ³⁶**For what use is it to gain all the wealth and power of this world, with everything it could offer you, at the cost of your own life?** ³⁷**And what could be more valuable to you than your own soul?** ³⁸**So among the unfaithful and sinful people living today, if you are ashamed of me and my words, the Son of Man will also be ashamed of you when he makes his appearance with his holy messengers**ᶜ **in the glorious splendor of his Father!"**ᵈ

---

a 8:34 Or "Follow me." This powerful verse was shocking to those who heard Jesus that day. To follow Jesus is more than the dethroning of our own lives, but the enthroning of Christ.

b 8:35 Or "will save it (his life)." There is only one Greek word for both "soul" and "life." The Aramaic uses a word that can mean "breath of life," "person," "soul," or "self."

c 8:38 Or "angels."

d 8:38 See Daniel 7:13–14.

$\mathcal{Nine}$

___

The Transfiguration of Jesus

¹Jesus said to them, **"I tell you the truth, there are some standing here now who won't experience death until they see God's kingdom realm manifest with power!"**ᵃ

²After six days, Jesus took Peter the Rock and the two brothers, Jacob and John, and hiked up a high mountain to be alone. And Jesus' appearance was dramatically altered, for he was transfigured before their very eyes! ³His clothing sparkled and became glistening white—whiter than any bleach in the world could make them. ⁴Then suddenly, right in front of them, Moses and Elijah appeared,ᵇ and they spoke with Jesus.

⁵Peter blurted out, "Beautiful Teacher,ᶜ *this is so amazing to see the three of you together! Why don't we stay here and set up*

___

a 9:1 This manifestation of the power of God's kingdom realm could be seen in three dimensions. 1) Beginning with verse 2, the kingdom power of God was seen in Jesus' transfiguration and the appearing of Moses and Elijah on the mountain. 2) Jesus' resurrection and ascension into glory inaugurated a new era of God's kingdom power. 3) The coming of the Holy Spirit at Pentecost, which brought to birth the church of Jesus Christ, and who extends God's kingdom realm to all the earth.

b 9:4 Moses represented the Law and Elijah represented the Prophets. Both Moses and Elijah were associated with Mount Sinai (Horeb), both had a ministry of performing astounding miracles, and both had unusual circumstances surrounding their passing from this life into glory. Peter tells us clearly that what he saw that day was a preview of God's kingdom realm (2 Peter 1:16–17).

c 9:5 Or "Good Rabbi," as translated from the Aramaic. *Rabbi* is an Aramaic title that means Master-Teacher.

three shelters:[a] one for you, one for Moses, and one for Elijah?" [6](For all of the disciples were in total fear, and Peter didn't have a clue what to say.) [7]Just then, a radiant cloud began to spread over them, enveloping them all. And God's voice suddenly spoke from the cloud, saying, **"This is my most dearly loved Son—always listen to him!"**[b]

[8]Suddenly, when they looked around, the disciples saw only Jesus, for Moses and Elijah had faded away.[c]

[9]As they all hiked down the mountain together, Jesus ordered them, **"Don't tell anyone of what you just witnessed. Wait until the Son of Man is raised from the dead."** [10]So they kept it to themselves, puzzled over what Jesus meant about rising from the dead.

[11]Then they asked him, "Why do the religious scholars insist that Elijah must come before the Messiah?[d]

[12]He answered them, **"They're right. Elijah must come first to put everything in order.[e] And what about all that is written about the Son of Man? It is true that he must endure many sufferings**

---

a 9:5 Or "booths," a reference to making booths for the Feast of Tabernacles. Peter wanted to celebrate that feast there on the mountaintop with Jesus, Moses, and Elijah. However, Jesus is not to be treated equally with Moses or Elijah—Jesus is the Lord of all creation, including all of humanity.

b 9:7 Or "You must constantly listen to him." See Deuteronomy 18:15, Psalm 2:7, and Isaiah 42:1.

c 9:8 Or "They saw no one with them anymore except Jesus." There were two mountains in the life of Jesus that focus on his true identity and mission. On this mountain, his face shined as bright as the sun; yet on Mount Calvary, his face was beaten to a pulp. On this mountain, his clothing was glistening white; yet on Mount Calvary, his clothing was taken from him and he was bleeding crimson. On this mountain, he had at his side two of the greatest men ever to live, Moses and Elijah; yet on Mount Calvary, he had at his side two murderers. On this mountain, the glory of God overshadowed him; yet on Mt. Calvary, he was alone, forsaken, in the dark. On this mountain, we hear the Father's voice of commendation; yet on Calvary's mountain, the Father was silent. How beautiful is Jesus on both mountains!

d 9:11 Or "come first (prior to the coming of the Messiah)."

e 9:12 See Malachi 4:5–6. Jesus is obviously referring to John the Immerser as the one who symbolized Elijah's coming. Using metaphors, symbols, and parables was Jesus' preferred way of teaching.

and be rejected.[a] [13]So Elijah has already appeared, just as it was prophesied,[b] and they did to him whatever they pleased."

The Disciples Unable to Cast Out a Demon

[14]Now when they came down the mountain to the other nine disciples, they noticed a large crowd of people gathered around them, with the religious scholars arguing with them. [15]The crowd was astonished to see Jesus himself walking toward them, so they immediately ran to welcome him.

[16]**"What are you arguing about with the religious scholars?"** he asked them.

[17]A man spoke up out of the crowd. "Teacher," he said, "I have a son possessed by a demon that makes him mute. I brought him here to you, Jesus. [18]Whenever the demon takes control of him, it knocks him down, and he foams at the mouth and gnashes his teeth, and his body becomes stiff as a board. I brought him to your disciples, hoping they could deliver him, but they were not strong enough."[c]

[19]Jesus said to the crowd, **"Why are you such a faithless people?[d] How much longer must I remain with you and put up with your unbelief? Now, bring the boy to me."**

[20]So they brought him to Jesus. As soon as the demon saw him, it threw the boy into convulsions. He fell to the ground, rolling around and foaming at the mouth [21]Jesus turned to the father and asked, **"How long has your son been tormented like this?"**

"Since childhood," he replied. [22]"It tries over and over to kill him

---

a 9:12 Read Psalm 22 and Isaiah 53.
b 9:13 Or "just as it was written about him."
c 9:18 That is, they were not able to conquer the demon.
d 9:19 Or "generation."

by throwing him into fire or water. But please, if you're able to do something, anything—have compassion on us and help us!"

²³Jesus said to him, **"What do you mean 'if'?**[a] **If you are able to believe,**[b] **all things are possible to the believer."**

²⁴When he heard this, the boy's father cried out with tears, saying, "I do believe, Lord; help my little faith!"[c]

²⁵Now when Jesus saw that the crowd was quickly growing larger, he commanded the demon, saying, **"Deaf and mute spirit, I command you to come out of him and never enter him again!"**

²⁶The demon shrieked and threw the boy into terrible seizures and finally came out of him! As the boy lay there, looking like a corpse, everyone thought he was dead. ²⁷But Jesus stooped down, gently took his hand, and raised him up to his feet, and he stood there completely set free![d]

²⁸Afterwards, when Jesus arrived at the house, his disciples asked him in private, "Why couldn't we cast out the demon?"

²⁹He answered them, **"This type of powerful spirit can only be cast out by fasting and prayer."**[e]

Jesus Again Prophesies of His Death and Resurrection

³⁰They went on from there and walked through the region of Galilee. Jesus didn't want the people to know he was there, because

---

a 9:23 Implied by the use of the most emphatic form of "if" in the Greek text.

b 9:23 As translated from the Aramaic and the majority of Greek manuscripts. There are, however, some Greek manuscripts that leave out the words "to believe."

c 9:24 As translated from the Aramaic. The Greek is "I do believe; help my unbelief."

d 9:27 Luke 9:43 adds "Everyone was awestruck. They were stunned seeing the power and majesty of God flow through Jesus."

e 9:29 As translated from the Aramaic and some Greek manuscripts. Many reliable Greek texts leave out "fasting." However, the word *fasting* was found on a fragment going back to the third century. (See also Isaiah 58:6.) Our lives must be saturated with the presence of God through prayer and fasting in order to conquer the evil that is in the world and hiding in the hearts of mankind.

he wanted to teach his disciples in private. [31]He said to them, **"The Son of Man is destined**[a] **to be betrayed and turned over to those who will execute him. But after three days he will rise again."** [32]But the disciples didn't have a clue what he meant and were too embarrassed to ask him to explain it.

The Disciples Argue Over Who Will Be the Greatest

[33]Then they came to Capernaum. And as soon as Jesus was inside the house, he asked his disciples, **"What were you arguing about on the way here?"**

[34]No one said a word, because they had been arguing about which one of them was the greatest. [35]Jesus sat down, called the twelve disciples to come around him, and said to them, **"If anyone wants to be first, he must be content to be last and become a servant to all."** [36]Then he had a child[b] come and stand among them. He wrapped the child in his arms and said to them, [37]**"Whoever welcomes a little child in my name welcomes me. And whoever welcomes me welcomes not only me, but the one who sent me."**

The Name of Christ

[38]John spoke up and said, "Teacher, we noticed someone[c] was using your name to cast out demons, so we tried to stop him because he wasn't one of our group."

[39]**"Don't stop him!"** Jesus replied. **"For the one who does miracles in the power of my name proves he is not my enemy.**[d] [40]**And**

---

a 9:31 The Greek verb, a futural present tense, implies something certainly meant to be.
b 9:36 The Greek word is not gender specific.
c 9:38 Some manuscripts add here "who does not follow along with us."
d 9:39 Or "would soon speak evil of me."

whoever is not against us is for us. 41Listen to the truth that I speak: Whoever gives you a cup of water because you carry the name of Christ will never lose his reward. 42But if anyone abuses*a* one of these little ones who believe in me, it would be better for him to have a heavy boulder*b* tied around his neck and be hurled into the deepest sea *than to face the punishment he deserves!* *c*

43"If your hand entices you to sin, let it go limp and useless!*d* For it is better for you to enter into life maimed than to have your entire body thrown into hell,*e* the place of unquenchable fire. 44This is where the maggots never die and the fire never goes out.*f* 45And if your foot leads you into sin, cut if off! For it is better to enter life crawling than to have both feet and be flung into hell. 46This is where the maggots never die and the fire never goes out. 47And if your eye causes you to sin, pluck it out! For it is better to enter into life with one eye than to be thrown into hell with two. 48This is where the maggots never die and the fire never goes out!*g*

49"Everyone will pass through the fire and every sacrifice will

---

a 9:42 Or "entraps, holds in bondage, enslaves, engages in child trafficking." The Aramaic is "confuses" or "misleads."

b 9:42 Or "the upper millstone turned by a donkey."

c 9:42 Implied in the words, "it would be better." Better than what? This is an ellipsis, which when made explicit, enhances the narrative. In the Hebrew text of Matthew 26:24 it reads, "It would be better for him not to even be born."

d 9:43 Or "Cut it off." Jesus is obviously using hyperbole to help us understand how purposeful we must be to guard our lives from sin.

e 9:43 Or "The Valley of Hinnom (Gehenna)," which is a metaphor for hell. Gehenna was known in the Old Testament era as the place where human sacrifice was offered to the pagan god Molech. See 2 Chronicles 33:6 and Jeremiah 7:31.

f 9:44 The oldest and most reliable manuscripts do not have verse 44 or verse 46. They are included in the Aramaic. See Isaiah 66:24.

g 9:48 The Aramaic can be translated "where their revenge never dies and their hatred does not subside."

be seasoned with salt.ª ⁵⁰Salt is excellent for seasoning. But if salt becomes tasteless,ᵇ how can its flavor ever be restored? Your lives, like salt, are to season and preserve.ᶜ *So don't lose your flavor,ᵈ* and preserve the peace in your union with one another."

---

a 9:49 As translated from the Aramaic and a few Greek manuscripts. The majority of reliable Greek texts have "Everyone will be salted with fire." Some manuscripts have "Every sacrifice will be salted with salt." Other manuscripts combine both statements, as does the Aramaic. The unbeliever will be thrown into the fires of Gehenna, and the believer will pass through the refining fire of God's holiness and love. The phrase "Every sacrifice will be seasoned with salt" may refer to us as "living sacrifices" who are made "salty" for God. In the days of Jesus, as soon as an animal was killed, it was salted to preserve the meat. See Leviticus 2:13 LXX, Malachi 3:2-3 and 4:1, and 1 Corinthians 3:11-15.

b 9:50 Or "loses its saltiness."

c 9:50 Or "Constantly have (hold) salt in yourselves"; that is, our lives are to become "salty" for God. Aramaic speakers refer to salt as a symbol of faithfulness in friendship. The Jews observed a "salt covenant." Jesus instructs his followers to be faithful friends to one another and to live in peace.

d 9:50 Implied by the comparison of salt losing its flavor and the disciples being like salt.

Ten

The Revolutionary Values of the Kingdom

¹Then Jesus left the region[a] and went into the district of Judea,[b] across from the Jordan River,[c] and again, massive crowds flocked to him, and Jesus, as was his custom, began to teach the people. ²At one point, some of the Pharisees came, seeking to entrap him with a question. "Tell us," they asked, "is it lawful for a man to divorce his wife?"

³He answered them, **"What did Moses command you?"**

⁴They replied, "Moses permitted us to write a certificate of separation that would be valid to complete a divorce."[d]

⁵Jesus said, **"Yes, Moses wrote this exception[e] for you because you are hardhearted. ⁶But from the beginning God created male**

---

a 10:1 Or "left that place (Capernaum, on the shore of Lake Galilee)."

b 10:1 Judea was a Roman province that included central Israel, with Jerusalem as its center. Jesus, leaving to go into Judea, began the journey he made to his destiny, to be crucified in Jerusalem.

c 10:1 The reason this is important to note is that this places Jesus in the jurisdiction of Herod Antipas, who had John the Immerser beheaded at the request of his stepdaughter. Now the Pharisees are coming to test Jesus in hopes of setting him up for likewise being put to death by Herod. The Aramaic notes the location as "the crossing place." This could have been the place where Joshua and the Hebrews crossed the Jordan to enter into the Promised Land.

d 10:4 See Deuteronomy 24:1 and Matthew 19:3–12. This question was asked in the context of an ongoing debate between two schools of rabbinical thought. The liberal view (Rabbi Hillel's) said that divorce could be made on any grounds, called "Any Matter" divorce, while the conservative viewpoint (Rabbi Shammai's) believed that divorce was only legal on the grounds of adultery. Jesus gave them God's view and used the creation of man and woman in the garden as the standard.

e 10:5 Or "commandment."

and female.ᵃ ⁷**For this reason a man will leave his parents and be wedded to his wife.**ᵇ ⁸**And the husband and wife**ᶜ **will be joined as one flesh, and after that they no longer exist as two, but one flesh.** ⁹**So there you have it. What God has joined together, no one has the right to split apart."**

¹⁰Once indoors, his disciples asked him to explain it to them again. ¹¹So he said to them, **"Whoever divorces his wife and marries another commits adultery against her.** ¹²**And if the wife divorces her husband and marries another, she also commits adultery.**

Jesus Blesses Little Children

¹³The parents kept bringing their little children to Jesus so that he would lay his hands on them *and bless them.*ᵈ But the disciples kept rebuking and scolding the people for doing it. ¹⁴When Jesus saw what was happening, he became indignant with his disciples and said to them, **"Let all the little children come to me and never hinder them! Don't you know that God's kingdom realm exists for such as these?** ¹⁵**Listen to the truth I speak: Whoever does not open their arms to receive God's kingdom like a teachable child will never enter it."**ᵉ ¹⁶Then he embraced each child, and laying his hands on them, he lovingly blessed each one.

---

a 10:6 See Genesis 1:27 and 5:2.

b 10:7 As translated from the Aramaic and the majority of Greek manuscripts. See Genesis 2:24 LXX.

c 10:8 Or "the two (i.e., husband and wife)."

d 10:13 Or "touch them." The laying on of Jesus' hands was an obvious impartation of a blessing. The words "and bless them," though implied, are made explicit in verse 16. Parents should always bring their children to be blessed by Jesus. The apparent reason for Mark including this episode is to express not only Jesus' desire to bless children, but also the disciple's inability to see people the way Jesus sees them.

e 10:15 Jesus uses an emphatic negative, something similar to "never, no never enter it."

A Rich Man Meets Jesus

17As Jesus started on his way, a man came running up to him. Kneeling down in from of him, he cried out, "Good Teacher, what one thing am I required to do to gain eternal life?"

18Jesus responded, **"Why do you call me good? Only God is truly good. 19You already know the commandments: 'Do not murder, do not commit adultery, do not steal, do not give a false testimony, do not cheat, and honor your father and mother.'"**[a]

20The man said to Jesus, "Teacher, I have carefully obeyed these laws since my youth."

21Jesus fixed his gaze upon the man, with tender love, and said to him, **"Yet there is still one thing in you lacking.**[b] **Go, sell all that you have and give the money to the poor. Then all of your treasure will be in heaven. After you've done this, come back and walk with me."**[c]

22Completely shocked by Jesus' answer, he turned and walked away very sad, for he was extremely rich.[d]

23Jesus looked at the faces of his disciples and said, **"How hard it is for the wealthy to enter into God's kingdom realm."**

24The disciples were startled when they heard this. But Jesus again said to them, **"Children, it is next to impossible for those who trust in their riches to find their way into God's kingdom realm.**[e]

---

a 10:19 See Exodus 20:12–16.

b 10:21 As translated from the Aramaic. The Greek is "You lack one thing." The Greek wording used here is the same as found in Romans 3:23, "We all are in need of (lack) the glory of God."

c 10:21 There are a few Greek and Aramaic manuscripts that read, "Pick up your cross."

d 10:22 Or "he had much property." The Greek word used here implies that he was a wealthy land owner.

e 10:24 Some reliable Greek manuscripts leave out the words "who trust in their riches." However, the majority of the Greek manuscripts and the Aramaic include it. The difficulty Jesus speaks of is not because it is evil to be rich, but because the wealthy are quick to put their confidence in riches and not in God. See 1 Timothy 6:9 and 17.

²⁵It is easier to stuff a rope through the eye of a needle[a] than for a wealthy person to enter into God's kingdom realm."[b]

²⁶But this left them all the more astonished, and they whispered to one another, "Then who could ever be saved?"

²⁷Jesus looked at them and replied, **"With people it is impossible, but not with God—God makes all things possible!"**[c]

²⁸Then Peter the Rock spoke up and said, "Can't you see that we've left everything we had to cling to you?"

²⁹**"Listen to my words,"** Jesus said. **"Anyone who leaves his home behind and chooses me over children, parents, family, and possessions, all for the sake of the gospel, ³⁰it will come back to him a hundred times as much in this lifetime—homes, family, mothers, brothers, sisters, children, possessions—along with persecutions. And in the age to come, he will inherit eternal life. ³¹But many who are considered to be the most important now will be the least important then. And many who are viewed as least important now will be considered the most important then."**

Jesus Again Prophesies of His Death and Resurrection

³²Jesus and his disciples were on the road that went up to Jerusalem, and Jesus was leading them forward. The disciples were filled with wonder and amazement at his bravery, but those following

---

a 10:25 As translated from the Aramaic. The Greek is "to stuff a camel through the eye of a needle." The Aramaic word for "rope" and for "camel" is the homonym *gamla*. This could be an instance of the Aramaic text being misread by the Greek translators as "camel" instead of "rope." Regardless, this becomes a metaphor for something impossible. It would be like saying, "It's as hard as making pigs fly!"

b 10:25 To enter into God's kingdom realm means more than salvation. It implies a participation in its principles and an experience of its power to change our hearts. The principles of God's kingdom are not the principles of the world. Greed is conquered by generosity. Promotion is given to the humble. The power of God's kingdom is found in the Holy Spirit. See Romans 14:17.

c 10:27 See Genesis 18:14 and Luke 1:37.

along with them were very afraid. As they approached the city, he took the twelve aside privately and told them what was going to happen. ³³**"I want you to know that we are going to Jerusalem, where the Son of Man will be handed over to the ruling priests and religious scholars and they will condemn him to death and hand him over to the Romans. ³⁴And they will mock him, spit in his face, torture him, and kill him, but three days later he will rise again."**

Jacob (James) and John Ask a Favor of Jesus

³⁵Jacob and John, sons of Zebedee, approached Jesus and said, "Teacher, will you do a favor for us?"ᵃ

³⁶**"What is it you're wanting me to do?"** he asked.

³⁷"We want to sit next to you when you come into your glory," they said, "one at your right hand and the other at your left."

³⁸Jesus said to them, **"You don't have a clue what you're asking for! Are you prepared to drink from the cup of suffering**ᵇ **that I am about to drink? And are you able to endure the baptism into death**ᶜ **that I am about to experience?"**

³⁹They replied, "Yes, we are able."ᵈ

Jesus said to them, **"You will certainly drink from the cup of my sufferings and be immersed into my death, ⁴⁰but to have you sit in**

---

a 10:35 A better question that followers of Jesus should ask is "What can we do to bring you glory? Anything you ask of us we will do for you if you will help us."

b 10:38 The cup is mentioned many times in the Old Testament as a metaphor of a cup of suffering. See Psalm 75:8, Isaiah 51:17–22, Jeremiah 25:15, and Ezekiel 23:31–34.

c 10:38 Baptism is a metaphor for immersion into death. See Romans 6:3–7, 1 Corinthians 10:2, and Colossians 2:11–13.

d 10:39 How naive was this for them to say! So many times we exaggerate our spirituality and believe we are more mature than we actually are. Yet in spite of their ambition and self-confidence, Jesus affirms that they will indeed taste of the sufferings of Christ.

the position of highest honor is not mine to decide. It is reserved for those whom grace has prepared them to have it."[a]

⁴¹Now the other ten disciples overheard this, and they became angry and began to criticize Jacob and John. ⁴²Jesus gathered them all together and said to them, **"Those recognized as rulers of the people and those who are in top leadership positions rule oppressively over their subjects, but this is not the example you are to follow. ⁴³You are to lead by a different model. If you want to be the greatest one, then live as one called to serve others. ⁴⁴The path to promotion and prominence comes by having the heart of a bond-slave**[b] **who serves everyone. ⁴⁵For even the Son of Man did not come expecting to be served by everyone, but to serve everyone, and to give his life as the ransom price in exchange for the salvation of many."**

Jesus Heals Blind Bar-Timai

⁴⁶When Jesus and his disciples had passed through Jericho, a large crowd joined them. Upon leaving the village, they met a blind beggar sitting on the side of the road named Timai, the son of Timai.[c]

---

a 10:40 As translated from the Aramaic. Mark's gospel records three times that Jesus prophesied of his death and resurrection. After each time he had to rebuke his disciples. The first time (Mark 8:31) he rebuked Peter for being used by Satan to try to hinder Jesus. The second time (Mark 9:31) the disciples argued over who would be the greatest. After the third time (Mark 10:33), Jesus corrected Jacob (James) and John about their ambition to be in the place of highest honor. This shows us that not only is the sacrifice of the cross difficult to understand, it also brings out the ambition that hides in our hearts. Jesus' submission to the Father to choose who sits in glory next to him becomes a rebuke to the ambition of James and John.

b 10:44 Jesus uses two Greek words for servant: *diakonos* ("minister, servant, deacon") in verse 43, and *doulos* ("bond-slave, bond-servant") in verse 44.

c 10:46 The name Timai is Aramaic and means "highly prized (esteemed)." Though unable to see, he was highly prized in the eyes of Jesus, who stopped to heal him. The Greek transliteration is "Bar-Timaeus, son of Timaeus," which is somewhat confusing, since the name Bar-Timaeus means "son of Timaeus." The Aramaic is correct; his name was Timaeus, named after his father, Timaeus. Timai spoke Aramaic when he cried out to Jesus, for "Rabbi" (Master-Teacher) is an Aramaic title of respect.

⁴⁷When he heard that Jesus from Nazareth was passing by, he began to shout "Jesus, son of David,ᵃ have mercy on me now in my affliction. *Heal me!*ᵇ"

⁴⁸Those in the crowd were indignant and scolded him for making so much of a disturbance, but he kept shouting with all his might, "Son of David, have mercy on me now *and heal me!*"

⁴⁹Jesus stopped and said, **"Call him to come to me."** So they went to the blind man and said, "Have courage! Get up! Jesus is calling for you!" ⁵⁰So he threw off his beggars' cloak, jumped up, and made his way to Jesus.

⁵¹Jesus said to him, **"What do you want me to do for you?"**

The man replied, "My Master,ᶜ please, let me see again!"

⁵²Jesus responded, **"Your faith heals you. Go in peace, with your sight restored."**ᵈ All at once, the man's eyes opened and he could see again, and he began at once to follow Jesus, walking down the road with him.

---

a 10:47 The term "Son of David" was used for the Messiah. The blind man believed Jesus was the one who was fulfilling the messianic claims of restoring sight to the blind.

b 10:47 Implied in the Hebraic saying "Have mercy on me." The mark of mercy would be his healing.

c 10:51 This is the Aramaic emphatic form of Rabbi: *Rabbouni.* "My Master" is the best way to express this in English.

d 10:52 This is the Greek word *sozo* and is best defined with multiple terms: "delivered, saved, restored, healed, rescued, preserved, made whole." There is at least an implication that the man was saved, healed, and delivered, with sight restored, all at the same time.

Eleven

Jesus' Triumphal Entry into Jerusalem

¹Now, as they were approaching Jerusalem, they arrived at the place of the stables[a] near Bethany on the Mount of Olives. Jesus sent two of his disciples ahead ²and said to them, **"As soon as you enter the village ahead, you will find a donkey's colt tethered there that has never been ridden. Untie it and bring it to me. ³And if anyone asks, 'Why are you taking it?' tell them, 'The master needs it and will send it back to you soon.'"[b]**

⁴So they went and found the colt outside in the street, tied to a gate. When they started to untie it, ⁵some people standing there said to them, "Why are untying that colt?"

⁶They answered just as Jesus had told them: *"The master needs it, and he will send it back to you soon."* So the bystanders let them go.[c]

---

a 11:1 Or Bethphage, which in Aramaic means "the house of stables." Transliterated into Greek it means "the house of unripe figs."

b 11:3 Only once in the Gospels do we see Jesus ever needing anything. In this case he needed a donkey. More than one commentator has seen a picture here of how the Lord "needs" every believer to be his representative in the world.

c 11:6 It is clear that Jesus had supernatural knowledge ahead of time about the colt, where it would be found, and what would be spoken by the bystanders. This would qualify as a "word of revelation knowledge," listed as one of the gifts of the Holy Spirit given to the church today. See 1 Corinthians 12:8. As the Creator, Jesus Christ has the right to be called the "owner" of the donkey.

⁷The disciples brought the colt to Jesus and piled their cloaks *and prayer shawls*ᵃ on the young donkey, and Jesus rode upon it.ᵇ ⁸Many people carpeted the road in front of him with their cloaks *and prayer shawls*,ᶜ while others gathered palm branches and spread them before him. ⁹Jesus rode *in the center* of the procession, with crowds going before him and behind him. They all shouted in celebration, "Bring the victory!ᵈ We welcome the one coming with the blessings of being sent from the Lord Yahweh!ᵉ ¹⁰Blessings rest on this kingdom he ushers in right now—the kingdom of our father David! Bring us the victory in the highest realms *of heaven!*"ᶠ

¹¹Jesus rode through the gates of Jerusalem and up to the temple. After looking around at everything, he left for Bethany with the twelve to spend the night, for it was already late in the day.

Jesus and a Fruitless Fig Tree

¹²The next day, as he left Bethany, Jesus was feeling hungry. ¹³He noticed a leafy fig tree in the distance, so he walked over to see if there was any fruit on it, but there was none—only leaves (for it

---

a 11:7 Or "garments." By cultural implication, this would include prayer shawls.

b 11:7 See Zechariah 9:9. Kings rode on horses, not donkeys. Jesus chose the young colt as a symbol of humility and gentleness. It would be difficult for the people to not see the fulfillment of Zechariah's prophecy in front of their eyes.

c 11:8 The men would have been wearing their prayer shawls as they welcomed Rabbi Jesus to Jerusalem. See also 2 Kings 9:13.

d 11:9 Or "Hosanna," an Aramaic word that means "O, save us now (bring the victory)!" The crowds were recognizing Jesus as Yahweh's Messiah. It is obvious that the people were expecting Jesus to immediately overthrow the Roman oppression and set the nation free. Many want victory before the cross, but true victory comes after resurrection.

e 11:9 As translated from the Aramaic. See Psalm 118:25–26.

f 11:10 Or "You who are in the highest place, save us now!"

wasn't yet the season for bearing figs).[a] [14]Jesus spoke[b] to the fig tree, saying, **"No one will ever eat fruit from you again!"** And the disciples overheard him.

Jesus Drives Merchants Out of the Temple Courts

[15]When they came into Jerusalem, Jesus went directly into the temple area and overturned all the tables and benches of the merchants who were doing business there. One by one he drove them all out of the temple courts,[c] and they scattered away, including the money changers[d] and those selling doves. [16]And he would not allow them to use the temple courts as a thoroughfare for carrying their merchandise and their furniture.

[17]Then he began to teach the people, saying, **"Does not the Scripture say, 'My house will be a house of prayer for all the world to share'?[e] But you have made it a thieves' hangout!"[f]**

[18]When the chief priests and religious scholars heard this, they began to hatch a plot as to how they could eliminate Jesus. But they feared him and his influence, because the entire crowd was carried away with astonishment by his teaching. [19]So he and his disciples spent the nights outside the city.

---

a 11:13 The fig tree is first mentioned in Genesis 3:7, with its leaves being a "covering" for fallen Adam and Eve to hide behind. It also became a hiding place for Zacchaeus, who climbed a sycamore-fig tree to see Jesus. The tree with leaves but no fruit can also be a symbol of Israel's religious system of that day (Jeremiah 8:13, 24:1–10). Jesus next drives out the money changers from the temple, which were rotten fruit. The firstfruits of the harvest Jesus was looking for came on the day of Pentecost, at the end of the Feast of Firstfruits. See Acts 2.

b 11:14 Or "Answering (the fig tree), he spoke to it." The text does not say that Jesus cursed the tree, only that he "answered" and spoke to the tree. Peter's interpretation of this was that Jesus cursed the tree (Mark 11:20–21).

c 11:15 Also known as the Court of the Gentiles, the only place where non-Jews were allowed in the temple complex.

d 11:16 The Aramaic reads, "the tables that had the firstborn ransom payments."

e 11:17 See Isaiah 56:7.

f 11:17 See Jeremiah 7:11.

Lessons of Faith

²⁰In the morning, they passed by the fig tree that Jesus spoke to and it was completely withered from the roots up. ²¹Peter the Rock remembered and said to him, "Teacher, look! That's the fig tree you cursed. It's now all shriveled up and dead."

²²Jesus replied, **"Let the faith of God be in you!ᵃ ²³Listen to the truth I speak to you: If someone says to this mountain with great faith and having no doubt:ᵇ 'Mountain, be lifted up and thrown into the midst of the sea,'ᶜ and believes that what he says will happen, it will be done. ²⁴This is the reason I urge you to boldly believe for whatever you ask for in prayer—believe that you have received it and it will be yours. ²⁵And whenever you stand praying,ᵈ if you find that you carry something in your heart against another person, release him and forgive himᵉ so that your Father in heaven will also release you and forgive you of your faults. ²⁶But if you will not release forgiveness, don't expect your Father in heaven to release you from your misdeeds."ᶠ**

---

a 11:22 As translated from the Aramaic. It is possible to translate the Greek text as an adjectival phrase, "God-like faith" or "godly faith."

b 11:23 The Aramaic word for *doubt* means "to be divided (undecided) in your heart."

c 11:23 The mountain and the sea can also be metaphors. Mountains in the Bible can refer to kingdoms, and the sea represents the nations (e.g., "sea of humanity"). Faith lifts up and brings with us the "mountain" of God's kingdom realm when we go into the nations. The Greek word for mountain, *oros*, is related to a verb that means "to lift up and carry off and take with you." This truth Jesus brings us is more than hyperbole; it is the active power of faith to take with us and carry the power and authority of the mountain-kingdom of God with us wherever we go.

d 11:25 Most ancient Jewish prayers require that a person stand to pray.

e 11:25 The Greek word for forgiveness is *apehiemi* and means "to send away, to take away, to release, to let flow (away)."

f 11:26 This verse is omitted by Nestle-Aland, Wescott & Hort, and most modern translations because it is not found in some of the most reliable and earliest manuscripts. It is found in the Aramaic. Although its inclusion is dubious, this translation includes it, for it does not interfere with the understanding of this pericope and a similar saying is found in Matthew 6:15.

The Religious Leaders Question Jesus' Authority

²⁷They came again into Jerusalem, and while Jesus was walking in the temple courts, the Jewish rulers—the chief priest, certain religious scholars, and the elders—approached him. They came up to him ²⁸and asked, "What right do you have to say and do these things? Who gave you the authority to do all this?"

²⁹Jesus replied, **"I too have a question to ask you. If you can answer this question, then I will tell you by what power I do all these things. ³⁰Where did John's authority to immerse come from? Was it from heaven or from people? Answer me now."**

³¹They stepped away and debated among themselves, saying, "How should we answer this? If we say from heaven, he will say to us, 'Then why didn't you respond to John and believe what he said?' ³²But if we say, 'From the people,' we fear the crowds, for they're convinced that John was God's prophet."

³³So they finally answered, "We don't know."

"Then neither will I tell you where my power comes from to do these things," Jesus replied.ᵃ

---

a 11:33 As they listened to the parable of the tenant in chapter 12, they began to understand that Jesus was the Son of God who came with heaven's authority to represent the Father.

The Parable of the Tenants

¹Then Jesus began to speak to them in parables: **"There once was a man who planted a vineyard[a] and put a secure fence around it.[b] He dug a pit for its winepress and erected a watch tower. Then he leased it to tenant-farmers and traveled abroad. ²When the time of harvest came, he sent one of his servants[c] to the tenants to collect the landowners' share of the harvest. ³But the tenants seized him and beat him and sent him back empty-handed. ⁴So the owner sent another servant to them. And that one they shamefully humiliated and beat over the head.[d] ⁵So he sent another servant, and they brutally killed him. Many more servants were sent, and they were all severely beaten or killed. ⁶The owner had only one person left to send—his only son, whom he dearly loved. So he sent him to them, saying, 'Surely they will restrain themselves[e] and respect my son.'**

---

a 12:1 The Aramaic can be translated "He planted a vineyard by a stream."

b 12:1 See Isaiah 5:1–7. The vineyard is a metaphor for the promises of life and glory for Israel. The leaders of the nation were but tenants who were to tend the vineyard. The fence was God's protection and favor that surrounded them. The winepress was the Holy Spirit, who gave them the inspired revelation of Scripture. The watchtower could speak of the ministry of the prophets, who were like watchmen on the walls for God's people.

c 12:2 These servants represent the prophets whom God commissioned to take his word to the people, but they were rejected and persecuted.

d 12:4 Some Greek manuscripts and the Aramaic read "and stoned him."

e 12:6 The Aramaic is "They'll be ashamed of what they've done."

⁷But the tenants *saw their chance* and said to one another, 'This is the heir. Come! Let's kill him, and then we'll inherit it all!' ⁸So they violently seized him, killed him, and threw his body over the fence!ᵃ ⁹So what do you think the owner of the vineyard will do? He will come and put to death those tenants and give his vineyard to others.ᵇ ¹⁰Haven't you read what the psalmist said?

> The stone the builders examined and rejected
>> has become the cornerstone,
>> the most important stone of all?ᶜ
> ¹¹This was the Lord's plan—
>> and heᵈ is wonderful for our eyes to behold!ᵉ

¹²Now, the chief priests, religious scholars, and leaders realized that Jesus' parable was aimed at them. They had hoped to arrest him then and there, but they feared the reaction of the crowd, so they left him alone and went away.

Paying Taxes to Caesar

¹³Then they sent a delegation of Pharisees, together with some staunch supporters of Herod, to entrap Jesus with his own words. ¹⁴So they approached him and said, "Teacher, we know that you're an honest man of integrity and you teach us the truth of God's ways. We can clearly see that you're not one who speaks only to win the people's favor, because you speak the truth without regard to the

---

a 12:8 Jesus was the true Heir, who was crucified outside the walls of the city. See Hebrews 13:12.

b 12:9 The "others" is a hint of the Gentiles who would receive the new covenant promises of God. See also John 15:1–2 and Ephesians 2:11–22.

c 12:10 See Psalm 118:22–23, Isaiah 8:14–15, and Isaiah 28:16.

d 12:11 Or "it."

e 12:11 The Aramaic reads, "This came from the presence of (next to) Lord Yahweh and is a marvel in our eyes."

consequences.[a] So tell us, then, what you think. Is it proper for us to pay taxes to Caesar or not?"

[15]Jesus saw through their hypocrisy and said to them, **"Why are you testing me? Show me one of the Roman coins."** [16]They brought him a silver coin used to pay the tax.

"Now, tell me," Jesus said, **"whose head is on this coin and whose inscription is stamped on it?"**

"Caesar's," they replied.[b]

[17]Jesus said, *"Precisely. The coin bears the image of the emperor Caesar, so you should pay the emperor his portion. But because you bear the image of God,[c] you must give back to God all that belongs to him."* And they were utterly stunned by Jesus' words.

A Question About Marriage

[18]Some of the Sadducees, a religious group that denied there was a resurrection of the dead, came to ask Jesus this question: [19]"Teacher, the law of Moses teaches[d] that if a man dies before he has children, his brother should marry the widow and raise up children for his brother's family line. [20]Now, there was a family with seven brothers. The oldest got married but soon died, and he had no children. [21]The second brother married his oldest brother's widow, and he also died without any children, and the third also. [22]This repeated down to the seventh brother, none of whom had children. Finally, the woman died. [23]So here's our dilemma: which of the seven brothers will be

---

a 12:14 Or "You don't look into the faces of men (before you speak the truth)."

b 12:16 Actual coins from that era have been found with the emperor's image and a superscription saying, "Tiberius Caesar Augustus, son of the divine Augustus."

c 12:17 Implied in the text. The coin belongs to Caesar because it carries his image. We have an obligation to God because we carry his image.

d 12:19 See Deuteronomy 25:5–10.

the woman's husband when she's resurrected from the dead, since they all were once married to her?"

²⁴Jesus answered them, **"You are deluded**ᵃ **because your hearts are not filled with the revelation of the Scriptures or the power of God.** ²⁵**For when they rise from the dead, men and women will not marry, just like the angels of heaven don't marry.** ²⁶**Now, concerning the resurrection, haven't you read in the Torah**ᵇ **what God said to Moses at the burning bush? 'I AM the Living God, the God of Abraham, the God of Isaac, and the God of Jacob'?**ᶜ ²⁷**God is not the God of the dead, but of the living, and you are all badly mistaken!"**ᵈ

The Greatest Commandment

²⁸Now a certain religious scholar overheard them debating. When he saw how beautifully Jesus answered all their questions, he posed one of his own, and asked him, "Teacher, which commandment is the greatest of all?"

²⁹Jesus answered him, **"The most important of all the commandments is this: 'The Lord Yahweh, our God, is one!'**ᵉ ³⁰**You are to love the Lord Yahweh, your God, with every passion of your heart, with all the energy of your being, with every thought that is within you, and with all your strength. This is the great and supreme commandment.** ³¹**And the second is this: 'You must love your neighbor**ᶠ

---

a 12:24 Or "You wander off the path (of truth)."

b 12:26 Or "in the book of Moses."

c 12:26 See Exodus 3:6. The implication Jesus is making is that Abraham, Isaac, and Jacob were all alive (in glory) when God spoke to Moses in the burning bush.

d 12:27 Or "You wander off the path (of truth)."

e 12:29 As translated from the Aramaic.

f 12:31 The Aramaic is literally "your nearest," which is a figure of speech for "your friend."

in the same way you love yourself.' You will never find a greater commandment than these."

³²The religious scholar replied, "Yes, that's true, Teacher. You spoke beautifully when you said that God is one, and there is no one else besides him.ᵃ ³³And there is something more important to God than all the sacrifices and burnt offerings: it's the commandment to constantly love God with every passion of your heart, with your every thought, and with all your strength—and to love your neighbor in the same way as you love yourself."

³⁴When Jesus noticed how thoughtfully and sincerely the man answered, he said to him, **"You're not far from the reality of God's kingdom realm."**ᵇ After that, no one dared to question him again.

Jesus, Son of David—Lord of David

³⁵While Jesus was teaching in the courts of the temple, he pos**ed a question to those listening: "Why do the religious scholars s**ay that the Messiah is David's son? ³⁶Yet it was David, inspired by the Holy Spirit, who sang:

> **The Lord Jehovah said to my Lord,**
> **"Sit near me in the place of authority**
> **until I subdue all your enemies under Your feet."**ᶜ
> ³⁷**"Since David calls him Lord, how can he be his son?"**

---

a 12:32 See Deuteronomy 4:35.

b 12:34 Jesus tells the man that God's kingdom realm is within reach. It is a present reality, not just a far-off concept. In Mark 11–12, the religious scholars (scribes) are mentioned a number of times. It was a religious scholar who questioned Jesus' authority (11:27–28), and it was a religious scholar who questioned his interpretation of Scripture (12:28). Now, in the verses that follow, Jesus shows that they had taught a theology without knowing the reality of Christ, the Messiah. Every teaching needs to be weighed by the reality of Christ, not the traditions of men.

c 12:36 See Psalm 110:1, the most quoted Old Testament verse found in the New Testament. Jesus is challenging them to consider that the Christ will be both God and man (David's son and David's Lord).

The large crowd that had gathered around Jesus took delight in hearing his words.

Jesus Warns Against the Religious Scholars

³⁸Jesus also taught the people, "Beware of the religious scholars.a They love to parade around in their clergy robes and be greeted with respect on the street.b ³⁹They crave to be made the leaders of synagogue councils,c and they push their way to the head table at banquets. ⁴⁰For appearance's sake, they will pray long religious prayers at the homes of widows for an offering, cheating them out of their very livelihood. Beware of them all, for they will one day be stripped of honor, and the judgment they receive will be severe."d

The Widow's Offering

⁴¹Then he sat down near the offering box, watching all the people dropping in their coins. Many of the rich would put in very large sums, ⁴²but a destitute widow walked up and dropped in two small copper coins, worth less than a penny. ⁴³Jesus called his disciples to gather around and then said to them, "I tell you the truth, this poor widow has given a larger offering than any of the wealthy. ⁴⁴For the rich only gave out of their surplus, but she sacrificed out of her poverty and gave to God all that she had to live on, which was everything she had."

---

a 12:38 The implied meaning of Jesus' teaching is that we should choose carefully those we follow. The religious scholars are not rebuked for their plans to crucify Jesus, but for their flawed character.

b 12:38 Or "marketplaces."

c 12:39 As translated from the Aramaic. The Greek is "the best seats (reserved for respected leaders) in the synagogues."

d 12:40 Translated from the Aramaic, which is literally "They eat of the household with the ladle of their tender prayers." The implication is that the religious leaders would go and pray at the homes of widows, then intimidate them by asking for offerings.

Thirteen

Jesus Prophesies the Destruction of the Temple

¹As Jesus was leaving the temple courts, one of his disciples came to him and said, "Teacher, look at these magnificent buildings! And what tremendous stones were used to build all this!"[a]

²Jesus turned to them and said, **"Take a good look at all these enormous buildings, for I'm telling you, there will not be one stone left upon another. It will all be leveled!"**[b]

Signs of the End of the Age

³Later, while Jesus was sitting on the Mount of Olives, overlooking the temple, his disciples, Peter the Rock, Jacob, John, and Andrew, came to him privately where he was sitting and said, ⁴"Tell us, when will these things happen? And what supernatural sign should we expect to signal your coming and the completion of this age?"[c]

---

a 13:1 This is Solomon's temple, rebuilt by Herod the Great. He began the project just prior to the birth of Christ in 19 BC, using some of the greatest marble and gold ornamentation found in the Middle East. Some of the stones he used were five meters long and over one meter high.

b 13:2 This prophecy of Jesus was fulfilled by the Roman prince Titus, who, in the Roman war of AD 67–70, destroyed the temple. There is still standing in Rome today the Arch of Titus, which commemorates his conquest of Jerusalem. In about AD 135, the emperor Hadrian completely destroyed the city of Jerusalem and built a new city on its foundations.

c 13:4 Although it is possible to translate this "the end of the world," the Hebraic mind-set of the end of days is a transition into a new age of the Messiah's coming that would restore all things. Note also that this teaching regarding the last days was not given publicly but only to four disciples.

⁵Jesus answered, "At that time deception will run rampant. So beware that you're not fooled! ⁶For many will appear on the scene claiming my authority* or saying about themselves, 'I am God's Anointed,'ᵇ and they will lead many astray. ⁷You will hear rumors of wars nearby, with more rumors of wars to come. Make sure that you are not thrown into a panic or give in to your fears, for these things are destined to happen. Prepare for it,ᶜ but still the end is not yet. ⁸For nationsᵈ will go to war against each other and kingdom against kingdom. And there will be terrible earthquakes in place after place—seismic events of epic proportion. And there will be famines and riots.ᵉ This is how the first contractions and birth pains of the new age will begin."

Jesus Warns of Persecution

⁹"Be on your guard! For they will repeatedly hand you over to the ruling councils, and you will be beaten in public gatherings. And you will stand trial before kings and high-ranking governmental leaders as an opportunity to testify to them on my behalf. ¹⁰*But prior to the end of the age,*ᶠ the hope of the gospelᵍ must first be preached to all nations.

¹¹"So when they put you under arrest and hand you over for trial, don't even give one thought about what you will say. Simply

---

a 13:6 Or "making use of my name."

b 13:6 Or "I am (the one)" or "It is I."

c 13:7 As translated from the Aramaic.

d 13:8 Or "ethnic groups." Although implied in the Greek, the Aramaic text is explicit: "Peoples will rise over peoples and kingdoms over kingdoms."

e 13:8 The word *riots* (rebellious uprisings) is found only in the Aramaic manuscripts. See also 2 Chronicles 15:6 and Isaiah 19:2.

f 13:10 The chronological reference ("first") takes us back to verse 7. That is, the end will not come before the gospel is preached to all nations.

g 13:10 As translated from the Aramaic (lit., "hopes").

speak what the Holy Spirit gives you at that very moment. And realize that it won't be you speaking but the Holy Spirit repeatedly speaking through you. ¹²Brothers will betray each other unto death—even a father his child. Children will rise up to take a stand against their parents and have them put to death. ¹³Expect to be hated by all because of your allegiance to the cause that bears my name. But determine to be faithful to the end and you will be saved."ᵃ

The Detestable Idol that Brings Misery

¹⁴When you witness what Daniel prophesied, 'the disgusting destroyer,'ᵇ standing where it must not beᶜ [Let the reader learn what it means],ᵈ then those in the land of Judah must escape to higher ground.ᵉ ¹⁵On that day, if you happen to be outside,ᶠ don't go back inside to gather your belongings. ¹⁶And if you're working out in the field, don't run back home to get a coat. ¹⁷It will be especially hardᵍ for pregnant women and for those nursing their babies when those days come. ¹⁸So pray that your escape will not be during the winter months. ¹⁹For this will be a time of great misery beyond the magnitude of anything the world has ever seen from the beginning of

---

a 13:13 Or "You will be rescued" or "preserved" or "delivered."

b 13:14 Or "the abomination (sin) that brings desolation (desecration)." See Daniel 8:13, 9:27, 11:31, and 12:11. Jesus is saying that Daniel's prophecy had not yet been fulfilled in his time. Many see the fulfillment of this prophecy in AD 70, when Titus, the Roman prince, went into the temple and sacrificed animals to Jupiter.

c 13:14 The Aramaic is "the defiling sign of desolation piling up (setting up)."

d 13:14 These parenthetical words were added by Mark to encourage us to seek the Lord for the understanding of this mystery. Jesus, speaking in the role of the true Prophet, gives us truth to ponder in veiled language.

e 13:14 See Jeremiah 16:16, Zechariah 14:5, and Luke 21:20–22.

f 13:15 Or "on the roof."

g 13:17 Or "woe." Jesus is not cursing them, but stating how dreadfully difficult it will be for them.

time[a] or ever will see. [20]Unless God limits those days, no one would escape. But because of his love for those chosen to be his, he will shorten that time of trouble.

[21]"And if you hear reports from people, saying, 'Look, the Messiah is over here,' or, 'The Messiah is over there!' don't believe it. [22]For there will be imposters falsely claiming to be God's 'Anointed One.' And false prophets[b] will arise to perform miracle signs, and if it were possible, they would cause God's chosen ones to wander off the right track. [23]Be alert, for I prophesy all this will happen!"

The Appearing of the Son of Man

[24]"This is what will take place after that suffering:

> The sun will be darkened and the moon will reflect no light.
> [25]The stars will be falling from the sky
> and all the cosmic powers will be shaken.[c]

[26]"Then they will see the Son of Man appearing in the midst of clouds and revealed with mighty power and great glory.[d] [27]At that time he will send his messengers,[e] who will gather together his beloved chosen ones from every direction—from the ends of the earth to the ends of heaven!"

---

a 13:19 Or "such as has not been seen from the beginning of the creation that God created until now."
b 13:22 The Aramaic is "prophets of lies."
c 13:25 See Isaiah 13:10, 34:4, Joel 2:10, and Amos 8:9. This can also be viewed as a Hebraic metaphor of the lights of the natural realm being shut off and replaced with heaven's glory. Lights out on the old order. Sun, moon, and stars are also representative of the governmental structures failing with great calamity. A new order, a new glory, is coming to replace the fading glories of this world.
d 13:26 See Daniel 7:13.
e 13:27 Or "angels." The Greek word for "angels" can also mean "messengers."

The Parable of the Fig Tree

28"Now, learn the lesson from the parable of the fig tree. When spring arrives, and it sends out its tender branches and sprouts leaves, you know that summer is soon to appear. 29So also, when you observe all these things progressively taking place, you will know that he[a] is coming near, even at the door! 30I assure you, this family[b] will not pass away until all I have spoken comes to pass. 31The earth and sky will wear out and fade away before one word I speak loses its power or fails to accomplish its purpose."

Live Always Ready for His Appearing

32"Concerning that day and exact hour, no one knows when it will arrive, not the angels of heaven, not even the Son—only the Father knows. 33This is why you must be waiting, watching and praying,[c] because no one knows when that season of time will come."

A Parable of a Man Who Left on a Journey

34"For those days can be compared to a man who was about to leave on a journey, but before leaving he placed his servants in charge and gave each one work to do while he was away. Then he commanded the watchman[d] to be on guard at all times. 35So I say to you, keep awake and alert—for you have no idea when the

---

a 13:29 Or "it."

b 13:30 As translated from the Aramaic, which employs a homonym that can be translated either "this generation will not pass away," or "this family will not pass away. The generation in which Jesus lived on earth has indeed passed away, but the Christian "family" of believers remains and endures. Arguably one of the most difficult verses in the Gospels to interpret, "this generation" could also refer to the Jewish people (race).

c 13:33 Most Greek manuscripts do not have "and praying"; however, there are ancient authorities who make reference to its inclusion here.

d 13:34 Or "doorkeeper."

master of the house will return; in the evening, at midnight, at four o'clock in the morning,[a] or at dawn. [36]Be alert, for he's coming suddenly and may find you sleeping! [37]And what I say to the four of you, I say to everyone—be awake at all times!"

---

a 13:35 Or "when the rooster crows."

Fourteen

The Plot To Kill Jesus

¹Two days before the Passover and the Feast of Unleavened Bread,ª the leading priests and religious scholars were committed to finding a way to secretly arrest Jesus and have him executed. ²But they all agreed that their plot could not succeed if they carried it out during the days of the feast, for they said, "There could be a riot among the people."

Jesus Is Anointed for His Death and Burial

³Now Jesus was in Bethany, in the home oᶠ Simon, a man Jesus had healed of leprᵒsy.b And as he was reclining at the table,c a woman came ᶦnto the house, holding an alabaster flask.d It was filled with

---

a 14:1 To commemorate the "passing over" of the death angel over the homes of the Hebrew people in Egypt, God instituted these days of celebration. It was an eight-day observance that began
with the Passover and included the Feast of Unleavened Bread. See Exodus 12:15–20 and 34:18.
Some believe there could have been 250,000 pilgrims who flocked to Jerusalem to observe the
celebrations. Jesus, our Passover Lamb, was killed on the Day of Passover.

b 14:3 We are all cleansed lepers, symbolized by Simon. Christ left the religious structure of the temple and went into the house of a leper. Former "lepers" are now the true temple of God.

c 14:3 In the times of Jesus, meals were not eaten sitting at a table, but rather while reclining on
one's side before a low table. There are two suppers mentioned in this chapter. At one, Jesus was
a guest; at the other, he was the host.

d 14:3 An alabaster flask would itself be considered a luxury item in that day. Alabaster was a type
of gypsum, very white and possibly translucent. It was found in caves and in limestone deposits.

the highest quality of fragrant and expensive oil.ª She walked right up to Jesus, and with a gesture of extreme devotion, she broke the flask and poured out the precious oil over his head. ⁴But some were highly indignant when they saw this, and they complained to one another, saying, "What a total waste! ⁵It could have been sold for a great sum,ᵇ and the money could have benefited the poor." So they scolded her harshly.

⁶Jesus said to them, **"Leave her alone! Why are you so critical of this woman? She has honored me with this beautiful act of kindness. ⁷For you will always have the poor, whom you can help whenever you want, but you will not always have me. ⁸When she poured the fragrant oil over me, she was preparing my body in advance of my burial.ᶜ She has done all that she could to honor me. ⁹I promise you that as this wonderful gospel spreads all over the world, the story of her lavish devotion to me will be mentioned in memory of her."ᵈ**

---

a 14:3 This was spikenard (or nard), a spice taken from a plant that grows in northern India near the Himalayas. This costly perfume would have been carried over land to the Middle East. Many believe this jar of spikenard would have cost the average worker a year's wages. It was a common practice among the Jews to prepare a body for burial with fragrant ointment. John records that it was about twelve ounces of perfume, which would have dripped down all of Jesus' garments to his feet (John 12:3).

b 14:5 Or "three hundred denarii," which is equivalent to nearly a year's salary. Works of charity are important, but they can never replace our devotion to Christ.

c 14:8 It is possible that when the Roman soldiers pierced Jesus' feet and placed the crown of thorns on his head, they could have smelled this fragrant oil.

d 14:9 Jesus' prophecy is that her sacrifice and love would be included in the gospel account. Her act of devotion is mentioned in three of the four gospels. You can't read the New Testament without knowing of her passionate act of worship. The gospel will always give birth to hearts filled with passion for Jesus.

Judas Schemes to Betray Jesus

¹⁰One of the twelve apostles, Judas Iscariot,ᵃ went to the leading priests to inform them of his willingness to betray Jesus into their hands. ¹¹They were delighted to hear this and agreed to pay him for it.ᵇ So immediately Judas began to look for an opportunity to betray him.

The Passover

¹²On the first day of Unleavened Bread, when the Passover Lamb is sacrificed, Jesus' disciples asked him, "Where would you like us to prepare the Passover mealᶜ for you?"

¹³So he sent two of his disciples ahead into Jerusalem with these instructions: **"Make your way into the city and watch for a man carrying an earthenware pitcher of water. Follow him, ¹⁴and say to the owner of whatever house he enters, 'The Teacher wants to ask you: "Do you have my room ready where I can eat the Passover meal with my disciples?"' ¹⁵And he will show you a large upstairs room ready and with a table set. Make preparations for us there."**

¹⁶So they went into the city and found everything to be exactly like Jesus had prophesied, and they prepared for him the Passover

---

a 14:10 Or "Judas the locksmith." Judas is the name Judah. Iscariot was not his last name. There are two possibilities for the meaning of Iscariot. Some believe it is taken from a Hebrew word that means "lock." Judah the locksmith. He most likely was the one who locked the collection bag, which means he had the key and could pilfer the fund at will. It's his sad history that he wanted to lock up Jesus and control him for his own ends. Other scholars see the possibility that Iscariot is actually "Ish (man) of Kerioth" (a town once situated south of Hebron). This would mean Judas was the only non-Galilean among the Twelve.

b 14:11 This was thirty pieces of silver, the going price of a slave. See Exodus 21:32 and Matthew 26:15.

c 14:12 That is, "the Passover seder."

meal.[a] [17]And when evening came, he entered the house and went upstairs with his twelve disciples. [18]Over dinner, while they were reclining around the table, Jesus said, **"Listen to the truth: one of you eating here with me is about to betray me."**

[19]Feeling deeply troubled by these words, one after another asked him, "You don't mean me, do you?"

[20]He answered, **"It is one of you twelve who has shared meals with me as an intimate friend.**[b] [21]**All that was prophesied of me, the Son of Man, is destined to soon take place,**[c] **but it will be disastrous for the one who betrays the Son of Man. It would be far better for him if he had never been born!"**

Jesus Shares Communion with His Twelve

[22]As they ate, Jesus took the bread and blessed it, tore it,[d] and gave it to his disciples. He said to them, **"Receive this; it is my body."** [23]Then taking the cup of wine and giving praises to the Father, he declared the new covenant with them.[e] And as each one drank from the cup,

---

a 14:16 This miracle account shows that Jesus had revelation knowledge and prophetic insight into the future. The disciples encountered the man, just like Jesus had said. Carrying water was a task given to women, making it easy to spot a man carrying a water jug. Also, it was somewhat of a miracle that during the feast days, with a quarter of a million pilgrims celebrating Passover in Jerusalem, there would be a large room like this unoccupied. This was the last Passover feast in God's economy, as the shadow of Passover was fulfilled at the cross, where Jesus was crucified. Passover is now replaced by the communion we share at the Lord's Supper. See 1 Corinthians 5:7-8.

b 14:20 Or "one who dips with me in the bowl." This is a figure of speech for an intimate friend.

c 14:21 Or "The Son of Man will go where it is written that he must go."

d 14:22 Although the Greek word *klao* means to "break bread," it is better understood as tearing a round loaf of flatbread in half. The symbolism of this communion meal was fulfilled by Jesus giving us his body on the cross. Jesus was not "broken" on the cross, but torn and distributed to each believer. We do not eat from a corpse; we feast on the glory of Christ's resurrected body, given now as the glory feast of the substance of Christ's glorified body.

e 14:23 As translated from the Aramaic.

²⁴he said to them, **"This is my blood, which seals the new**ᵃ **covenant poured out for many.** ²⁵**I tell you the truth, I will not drink again of the fruit of the vine until the day comes when we drink it together in the kingdom realm of my Father."**ᵇ ²⁶Then they sang a psalmᶜ and afterwards left for the Mount of Olives.

Jesus Prophesies of Peter's Denial

²⁷Jesus said to them, **"You will all fall away and desert me.**ᵈ **This will fulfill the prophecy of the Scripture that says:**

> **I will strike down the shepherd
> and all the sheep will scatter far and wide.**ᵉ

²⁸**"But after I am risen,**ᶠ **I will go ahead of you to Galilee."**

²⁹Then Peter the Rock spoke up and said, "Even if all the rest lose their faith and fall away, I will still be beside you, Jesus!"

³⁰Jesus said, **"Mark my words, Peter. This very night, before the**

---

a 14:24 A few Greek manuscripts do not have the word *new*. It is included in the Aramaic and the majority of Greek texts. This new covenant is a better covenant because it is established on better promises. In this new covenant, God freely gives us forgiveness, life, salvation, and every heavenly spiritual blessing. See Ephesians 1:3 and Hebrews 8:6–13 and 9:16–17. Jesus serves his disciples the bread, the cup, and the blood (wine), which means he is serving us his death and resurrection, which now is our feast and our constant supply of life (John 6:51).

b 14:25 We are now in the realm of the kingdom of God. The Holy Spirit brings us into the body of Christ and into the reality of God's kingdom realm. It is growing and increasing in scope, and every time believers drink of the cup of communion, Jesus is present with us. It is the Lord's Table, not ours. This was a prophecy of what would happen in just a matter of days from then, as believers would break bread together in remembrance of what Jesus did for each of us. See Acts 2:42. Jesus now drinks it with us in a new way, and not just once a year at Passover, but every time we worship him by taking communion.

c 14:26 Or "a hymn." The Aramaic is "They offered praise." It was the custom after celebrating the Passover seder to conclude with singing one of the Hallel psalms (115–118).

d 14:27 Or "You will all fall into a trap and be ensnared."

e 14:27 See Zechariah 13:7.

f 14:28 Jesus knew he would triumph over death and be raised from the dead.

rooster crows twice a few hours from now, you will utterly deny that you know me three times."

[31]But Peter was insistent and replied emphatically, "I will absolutely not! Under no circumstances will I ever deny you—even if I have to die with you!" And all the others repeated the same thing.

Jesus Prays in Gethsemane

[32]Then Jesus led his disciples to an orchard called "The Oil Press."[a] He told them, **"Sit here while I pray awhile."** [33]He took Peter, Jacob, and John with him.[b] An intense feeling of great horror plunged his soul into deep sorrow and agony. [34]And he said to them, **"My heart is overwhelmed with anguish and crushed with grief.[c] It feels as though I'm dying. Stay here and keep watch with me."**

[35]He walked a short distance away, and being overcome with grief, he threw himself facedown on the ground. He prayed that if it were possible, he would not have to experience this hour *of suffering.* [36]He prayed, **"Abba, my Father, all things are possible**

---

a 14:32 Or "Gethsemane," the Aramaic word for "(olive) oil press." This was located on the lower slope of the Mount of Olives near the brook Kidron. King David left Jerusalem weeping as he crossed the Kidron Valley and went up the Mount of Olives (2 Samuel 15:23). Now the Son of David comes into that valley with great sorrow on his way into Jerusalem to be crucified. Kidron comes from the Hebrew verb *qadar*, which means "to grow dark" or "to mourn."

b 14:33 Peter, Jacob (James), and John were the three disciples who were witnesses of Christ's glory when he was transfigured before their eyes. On the eve of his crucifixion, Jesus longed to have his three closest disciples nearby.

c 14:34 The Greek words used here in verses 33–34 are unusual. The terms are extraordinarily emotional and expressive, describing the deepest feelings a person could experience.

for you. Please—don't allow me to drink this cup of suffering!ᵃ Yet what I want is not important, for I only desire to fulfill your plan for me."

³⁷Then he came back to his three disciples and found them all sound asleep. He awakened Peter and said to him, **"Simon, are you asleep? Do you lack the strength to stay awake with me for even just an hour? ³⁸Keep alert and pray that you'll be spared from this time of testing. For your spirit is eager enough, but your humanity is feeble."**ᵇ

³⁹Then he left them a second time and went to pray the same thing. ⁴⁰Afterward, he came back to the disciples and found them sound asleep, for they couldn't keep their eyes open and they didn't know what to say to him.

⁴¹After praying for the third time, he returned to his disciples and awoke them again, saying, **"Do you plan on sleeping and resting indefinitely? That's enough sleep! The end has come and the hour has arrived**ᶜ **for the Son of Man to be handed over to the authority of sinful men. ⁴²Get up and let's go. Don't you see? My betrayer draws near."**

---

a 14:36 The cup becomes a metaphor of the great suffering that Jesus had to endure that night in the garden. However, Jesus was not asking the Father for a way around the cross. Rather, he was asking God to keep him alive through this night of suffering so that he could carry the cross and take away our sins. According to the prophecies of the Old Testament, Jesus was to be pierced on a cross. We learn from Hebrews 5:7 that Jesus' prayer was answered that night as the cup was indeed taken from him. An angel of God came to strengthen him and deliver him from premature death (Matthew 26:39). The "cup" he was asking God to let pass from him was the cup of premature death that Satan was trying to make him drink in the garden, not the death he would experience the next day on the cross. He had already sweat drops of blood (Luke 22:44), but the prophecies had to be fulfilled of being pierced on a cross for our transgressions. God answered his cry and he lived through the agony of Gethsemane so that he could be our sacrifice for sin on Calvary. Jesus did not waver in the garden. We have a brave Savior.

b 14:38 The Aramaic is "The flesh is failing."

c 14:41 Or "It is received in full; the hour has come." Although this clause is not found in the most reliable Greek texts, it is included in the Aramaic and a few Greek manuscripts (Codex D).

Jesus' Betrayal and Arrest

⁴³At that moment Judas, one of the Twelve, arrived, along with a large crowd of men armed with swords and clubs. They had been sent to arrest Jesus by order of the ruling priests, the religious scholars, and the Jewish leaders. ⁴⁴Now, Judas, the traitor, had arranged to give them a signal that would identify Jesus, for he had told them, "Jesus is the man I will kiss. So grab him and take him safely away." ⁴⁵Judas quickly stepped up to Jesus and said, "Rabbi, my Teacher!"ᵃ and he kissed him affectionately on both cheeks.

⁴⁶Then the armed men seized Jesus to arrest him. ⁴⁷One of the disciplesᵇ pulled out a swordᶜ and swung it at the servant of *Caiaphas*, the high priest, slashing off his ear.

⁴⁸Jesus said to the mob, **"Why would you arrest me with swords and clubs as though I were an outlaw?ᵈ ⁴⁹Day after day I sat with you in the temple courts, teaching the people, yet you didn't arrest me then. But all of this fulfills the prophecies of the Scriptures."** ⁵⁰At that point all of his disciples ran away and abandoned him.

⁵¹There was a young manᵉ there following Jesus, wearing only a linen sheet wrapped around him.ᶠ ⁵²They tried to arrest him also,

---

a 14:45 The Aramaic repeats Rabbi (my Teacher); the Greek has it only once.

b 14:47 Or "bystanders," which we know to have included Peter. See John 18:10.

c 14:47 This was a small sword or dagger.

d 14:48 Or "revolutionary."

e 14:51 Traditionally, this young man was thought to be Mark, the author of this gospel. Mark may be using the common literary device of allusion when speaking of himself. The Greek text uses the word *neaniskos*, which would mean that the young man was a teenager or in his early twenties.

f 14:51 This linen sheet is from the Greek word *sindon* and occurs in the Synoptic Gospels to describe the linen sheet used for burial cloth. *Sindon* is also used for the young man (*neaniskos*) dressed in linen who announced to the women at the tomb that Jesus was alive (Mark 16:5–7). This event can also be seen as a foreshadowing of the resurrection, with the symbolism of the burial cloth and escape from their clutches.

but he slipped from their grasp and ran off naked,[a] leaving his linen cloth in their hands.

Jesus Condemned by the Religious Leaders

⁵³Those who arrested Jesus led him away to Caiaphas, the high priest, to a meeting where the religious scholars and Jewish leaders were assembled. ⁵⁴Now, Peter the Rock had followed him from a distance all the way to the chief priest's courtyard. He sat with the guards and was warming himself by the fire.

⁵⁵The chief priests and the entire supreme Jewish council of leaders were doing their best to find false charges that they could bring against Jesus and condemn him to death, but they could not find any. ⁵⁶Many false witnesses came forward, but the evidence could not be corroborated. ⁵⁷Some came forward and testified against him, saying, ⁵⁸"We heard him say, 'I can destroy this temple made with hands and then build another one again in three days not made with hands!'" ⁵⁹Yet even on this point the witnesses did not agree.

⁶⁰Finally, the chief priest stood up in the middle of them and said to Jesus, "Have you nothing to say about these allegations? Is what they're saying about you true?"

⁶¹But Jesus remained silent before them and did not answer. So the chief priest said to him, "Are you the anointed Messiah, the Son of the Blessed God?"

⁶²Jesus answered him, **"I AM! And more than that, you are about**

---

a 14:51 Or "he was nearly naked," for in the Jewish culture, if you were in your undergarment, you were considered to be naked. The linen garment (tunic) would point to a family of wealth. We know the weather was somewhat cold that night, for in just a few hours Peter would be standing by a fire, warming his hands.

to see the Son of Man seated at the right hand of the Almighty and coming in the heavenly clouds!"[a]

[63]Then, *as an act of outrage,* the high priest[b] tore his robe and shouted, "No more witnesses are needed, [64]for you've heard this grievous blasphemy." *Turning to the council he said,* "Now, what is your verdict?"

"He's guilty and deserves the death penalty!" they all answered.

[65]Then they spat on his face[c] and blindfolded him. Others struck him over and over with their fists and taunted him by saying, "Prophesy to us! *Tell us which one of us is about to hit you next?"* And the guards took him and beat him.

Peter's Denials

[66]Meanwhile, Peter the Rock was sitting below in the courtyard when a girl, a servant of the high priest, came near the fire. [67]When she saw Peter there warming himself, she said to him, "I recognize you. You were with that Nazarene, Jesus."

[68]But Peter denied it, saying, "I don't have a clue what you're talking about." Then he went out to the gateway of the courtyard and the rooster crowed.[d]

[69]When the servant girl noticed him, she said to all the bystanders, "I know this man is one of his followers!"

[70]Once again, Peter denied it. A short time later, the bystanders

---

a 14:62 See Daniel 7:13.

b 14:63 What a dramatic scene! Two high priests are facing each other: the high priest of the Jewish system and the true High Priest. One is of the order of Aaron; the other of the order of Melchizedek (Hebrews 7:11–28). One a sinful man; the other, the sinless Son of God. It is clear from Leviticus 21:10 that if a high priest tears his robe he is disqualified from his office. Indeed, Caiaphas is now stepping aside and God's true High Priest is taking his place.

c 14:65 See Isaiah 50:6.

d 14:68 Some manuscripts leave out the last phrase, "and the rooster crowed."

said to him, "You must be one of them. You're a Galilean, like he is, for your accent proves it!"[a]

⁷¹Peter the Rock cursed and said, "I tell you, I don't know this man you're talking about!"

⁷²At the same moment Peter spoke those words, the sound of a rooster crowing pierced the night for the second time. And Peter remembered the words Jesus had spoken to him earlier: **"Before the rooster crows twice, you will deny me three times."** *With a shattered heart,* Peter the Rock broke down and sobbed with bitter tears.

---

a 14:70 Or "You are also a Galilean." As a Galilean, Peter spoke a northern dialect of Aramaic that would pronounce certain words slightly differently, much like English is spoken with different accents around the world.

Jesus Handed Over to Pilate

¹Before dawn that morning, all the ruling priests, elders, religious scholars, and the entire Jewish council set in motion their plan against Jesus. They bound him in chains, took him away, and handed him over to Pilate.

²*As Jesus stood in front of the Roman governor,*ᵃ Pilate asked him, "So, are you really the king of the Jews?"

Jesus answered, **"You have just spoken it."**

³Then the ruling priests, over and over, made bitter accusations against him, but he remained silent.ᵇ

⁴So Pilate questioned him again. "Have you nothing to say? Don't you hear these many allegations they're making against you?" ⁵But Jesus offered no defense to any of the charges, much to the great astonishment of Pilate.

Jesus and Barabbas

⁶Every year at Passover, it was the custom of the governor to pardon a prisoner and release him to the people—anyone they wanted.

---

a 15:2 The Aramaic identifies him as the Roman governor; the Greek is simply Pilate.
b 15:3 See Isaiah 53:7 and 1 Peter 2:23.

⁷Now, Pilate was holding in custody a notorious criminal named Bar-Abbas,ᵃ one of the assassinsᵇ who had committed murder in an uprising. ⁸The crowds gathered in front of Pilate's judgment bench and asked him to release a prisoner to them, as was his custom.

⁹So he asked them, "Do you want me to release to you today the king of the Jews?" ¹⁰(Pilate was fully aware that the religious leaders had handed Jesus over to him because of sheer spite and envy.)

¹¹But the ruling priests stirred up the crowd to incite them to ask for Barabbas instead.

¹²So Pilate asked them, "Then what do you want me to do with this one you call the king of the Jews?"

¹³They all shouted back, "Crucify him!"

¹⁴"Why?" Pilate asked. "What evil thing has he done wrong?" But they kept shouting out with an deafening roar, "Crucify him at once!"

¹⁵Because he wanted to please the people, Pilate released Barabbas to them. After he had Jesus severely beaten with a whip made of leather straps *and embedded with metal,*ᶜ he sentenced him to be crucified.ᵈ

---

a 15:7 The name Bar-Abbas is Aramaic and means "son of a father" or "son who is like his father." He becomes a picture of every son of Adam, our father. The true Son of the Father was crucified that day. One man wanted a political revolution, the other a revolution of love filling the hearts of all men.

b 15:7 As translated from the Aramaic. The Greek is "revolutionaries."

c 15:15 This was a tortuous beating with a leather whip that had sharp pieces of bone and metal at the end of its lashes, designed to inflict severe pain.

d 15:15 The Jewish death penalty was by stoning. It was the Roman practice to crucify only rebellious slaves and the worst of criminals. To have Jesus crucified was not only the fulfillment of Old Testament prophecies (Galatians 3:13; Isaiah 53:5–8) but also the fulfillment of Jesus' own words concerning the mode of his death (John 3:14, 8:28, 12:32), which would not have been fulfilled by stoning.

The Soldiers Mock Jesus

¹⁶The soldiers took Jesus into the headquarters of the governor's compound[a] and summoned a military unit of nearly six hundred men.[b] ¹⁷They placed a purple robe on him *to make fun of him.* Then they braided a victor's crown, a wreath made of thorns,[c] and set it on his head. ¹⁸And with a mock salute they repeatedly cried out, "Hail, your majesty, king of the Jews!" ¹⁹They kept on spitting in his face and hit him repeatedly on his head with a reed staff, driving the crown of thorns deep into his brow. They knelt down before him in mockery, pretending to pay him homage. ²⁰When they finished ridiculing him, they took off the purple robe, put his own clothes back on him, and led him away to be crucified.

The Crucifixion of Jesus

²¹As they came out of the city, they stopped an African man named Simon, a native of Libya.[d] He was passing by, just coming in from the countryside with his two sons,[e] Alexander and Rufus, and the soldiers forced him to carry the heavy crossbeam for Jesus. ²²They brought Jesus to the execution site called Golgotha, which means

---

a 15:16 Or "praetorium."

b 15:16 That is, a Roman cohort (battalion), which was the tenth part of a Roman legion of about six thousand men.

c 15:17 Thorns are an emblem of the curse of sin. Jesus took the curse for us. See Genesis 3:17–18 and Galatians 3:13.

d 15:21 Or "from Cyrene," which is present-day Tripoli, Libya. Cyrene was a Greek colony that had a great number of Jews who had been forced to live there during the reign of Ptolemy Soter (323–285 BC). Church tradition states that Simon's two sons became powerful missionaries for Jesus Christ. Their mention here might indicate that they were notable among the early Christians. See Romans 16:13. It is also possible that Simon himself could be linked to the "believers from Cyprus and Cyrene" who were evangelists to the Syrians, mentioned in Acts 11:20.

e 15:21 Or "the father of two sons," who, by implication, were with him at that time. Church tradition states that their names were Rufus and Alexander who became missionaries preaching the message of Christ. See Romans 16:13.

"Skull Hill."ᵃ ²³There they offered him a mild painkiller, a drink of wine mixed with gall,ᵇ but he refused to drink it.

²⁴They nailed his hands and feet to the cross. The soldiers divided his clothing among themselves by rolling diceᶜ to see who would win them. ²⁵It was nine o'clock in the morningᵈ when they finally crucified him. ²⁶Above his head they placed a sign with the inscription of the charge against him, which read, "This is the King of the Jews."

²⁷Two criminals were also crucified with Jesus, one on each side of him. ²⁸This fulfilled the Scripture that says:

He was considered to be a criminal.ᵉ

²⁹Those who passed by shook their heads and spitefully ridiculed him, saying, "Aha! You boasted that you could destroy the temple and rebuild it in three days.ᶠ ³⁰Why don't you save yourself now? Just come down from the cross!"

³¹Even the ruling priests and the religious scholars joined in the mockeryᵍ and kept laughing among themselves,ʰ saying, "He saved others, but he can't even save himself! Israel's king, is he? ³²Let the 'Messiah,' the 'king of Israel,' *pull out the nails and* come down from the cross right now. We'll believe it when we see it!" Even the two

---

a 15:22 The Aramaic word is Golgotha (Mark uses a variant dialectic form, Gajultha). This is *calvaria* in Latin, or "Calvary." David took Goliath's head (Goliath and Golgatha are taken from the same root word) and buried it outside of Jerusalem. Some believe this is where the hill got its name, Golgotha (the place of the skull). The cross has to pierce the place of the skull for our minds to submit to the revelation of the cross.

b 15:23 See Psalm 69:21.

c 15:24 That is, they cast lots. See Psalm 22:18.

d 15:25 Or "the third hour (of the day)."

e 15:28 See Isaiah 53:12. Although this verse is not found in some of the early and reliable Greek manuscripts, the majority of manuscripts do include it, and it is also found in the Aramaic.

f 15:29 Jesus never said that he would destroy the temple, but that it would be destroyed by others.

g 15:31 See Psalm 22:17, Psalm 109:25, and Lamentations 2:15.

h 15:31 As translated from the Aramaic.

criminals who were crucified with Jesus began to taunt him, hurling insults on him.

The Death of Jesus

[33]For three hours, beginning at noon, darkness came over the earth.[a] [34]About three o'clock, Jesus shouted with a mighty voice in Aramaic,[b] **"Eli, Eli, lama sabachthani?"**—that is, **"My God, My God, why have you turned your back on me?"**[c]

[35]Some who were standing near the cross *misunderstood* and said, "Listen! He's calling for Elijah."[d] [36]One bystander ran and got a sponge, soaked it with sour wine, then put it on a stick and held it up for Jesus to drink.[e] But the rest said, "Leave him alone! Let's see if Elijah comes to rescue him." [37]Just then Jesus passionately cried out with a loud voice and breathed his last.[f] [38]At that moment the veil *in the Holy of Holies* was torn in two from the top to the bottom.[g]

[39]When the Roman military officer who was standing right in front of Jesus saw how he died, he said, "There is no doubt this man was the Son of God!

[40-41]Watching from a distance, *away from the crowds*, were many of the women who had followed Jesus from Galilee and had

---

a 15:33 See Exodus 10:22, Amos 8:9–10, Joel 2:30-31, and Acts 2:16–21.

b 15:34 The last words of Jesus were spoken in Aramaic. Every Greek text gives a transliteration of the Aramaic words and then translates them back into Greek.

c 15:34 See Psalms 22:1 and 42:9. The Aramaic can be translated "For this purpose you have spared me."

d 15:35 Perhaps they misunderstood because the Aramaic word *Eli* sounds similar to the name Elijah.

e 15:36 See Psalm 69:21.

f 15:37 See Luke 23:46 and John 19:30 to read the words he shouted out at death.

g 15:38 The veil torn from the top to the bottom proves that it was God who did this, for the veil was very thick, heavy, and nearly eighty feet tall. See Hebrews 10:19–22.

cared for him.[a] Among them were Miriam Magdalene,[b] Miriam the mother of Jacob the younger[c] and Joseph,[d] and Salome. Many other women who had followed him to Jerusalem were there too.[e]

Jesus' Burial

[42]Evening was fast approaching, and it was a preparation day before a Sabbath. [43]So a prominent Jewish leader named Joseph, from the village of Ramah,[f] courageously went to see Pilate and asked to have custody of the body of Jesus. Joseph was a highly regarded member of the Jewish council and a follower of Jesus[g] who had focused his hope on God's kingdom realm.[h] [44]Pilate was amazed to hear that Jesus was already dead, so he summoned the Roman officer, who confirmed it.[i] [45]After it was confirmed, Pilate consented to give the corpse to Joseph.

[46]Joseph purchased a shroud of fine linen and took the body down from the cross. Then he wrapped it in the linen shroud and placed it in a tomb quarried from out of the rock.[j] Then they rolled a large stone over the entrance to seal the tomb. [47]Miriam Magdalene

---

a 15:40-41 Or "ministered to him." This most likely included financial support.

b 15:40-41 Or "Miriam of (the village of) Magdala," which was recently discovered on the south-western shore of the Lake of Galilee. See also Luke 8:2.

c 15:40-41 Or "James, the short one."

d 15:40-41 Or "Joses," a nickname for Joseph that perhaps could best be translated "Joey."

e 15:40-41 Apparently, all the men had fled from the scene except for the apostle John. See John 19:26.

f 15:43 As translated from the Aramaic. Ramah (formerly Ramathaim Zophim) was the village of Samuel, situated on a hill overlooking Jerusalem. The Greek is "Joseph of Arimathea." Luke tells us that he was a member of the Sanhedrin. See Luke 23:50–51. It is possible that Joseph may have lost a son the age of Jesus when Herod killed the infants.

g 15:43 See Matthew 27:57.

h 15:43 The Greek text could be translated "He was habitually focusing and progressively moving toward receiving (welcoming, anticipating) God's kingdom reign." The Aramaic is "anxiously await-ing the kingdom realm of God."

i 15:44 Or "if he had died too soon."

j 15:46 This was a tomb that had been chiseled into a rock, forming a cave-like structure.

and Miriam the mother of Joseph[a] were there and saw exactly where they laid the body of Jesus.

---

a 15:47 Or "Joses."

Sixteen

The Resurrection of Jesus

1-2On the first day of the week, as the Sabbath was ending, Miriam Magdalene, Miriam the mother of Jacob, and Salome made their way to the tomb. It was very early in the morning as the first streaks of light were beginning to be seen in the sky. They had purchased aromatic embalming spices so that they might anoint his body. 3And they had been asking one another, "Who can roll away the heavy stone for us from the entrance of the tomb?" 4But when they arrived, they discovered that the very large stone that had sealed the tomb was already rolled away! 5And as they stepped into the tomb, they saw a young man sitting on the right, dressed in a long white robe. The women were startled and amazed. 6But the angel*a* said to them, "Don't be afraid. I know that you're here looking for Jesus of Nazareth, who was crucified. He isn't here—he has risen victoriously! Look! See the place where they laid him. 7Run and tell his disciples, even Peter the Rock, that he is risen. He has gone ahead of you into Galilee and you will see him there, just like he told you."

8They staggered out of the tomb, awestruck,*b* with their minds

---

a 16:6 See Matthew 28:2.
b 16:8 Or "trembling (with astonishment)."

swirling. They ran to tell the disciples, but they were so afraid and deep in wonder, they said nothing to anyone.[a]

Jesus Appears to Some of His Followers

[9]Early on the first day of the week, after rising from the dead, Jesus appeared to Miriam Magdalene, from whom he had cast out seven demons. [10]After she had seen Jesus, she ran to tell his disciples, who were all emotionally devastated and weeping. [11]Excitedly, Miriam told them, "He's alive and I've seen him!" But even after hearing this, they didn't believe her.

[12]After this, Jesus appeared to two of the disciples, who were on their way to another village,[b] appearing in a form they did not recognize. [13]They went back *to Jerusalem* to tell the rest of the disciples, but they didn't believe it was true.

[14]Then Jesus appeared[c] before the eleven apostles as they were eating a meal. He corrected them for having such hard, unbelieving hearts because they did not believe those who saw him after his resurrection.

[15]And he said to them, **"As you go into all the world, preach openly the wonderful news of the gospel to the entire human race! [16]Whoever believes the good news and is baptized will be saved, and whoever does not believe the good news will be condemned. [17]And these miracle signs will accompany those who believe: They**

---

a 16:8 Some early manuscripts of Mark do not include verses 9–20. They are found in the Aramaic. A shorter ending to Mark found in a few manuscripts reads, "They reported briefly to those around Peter all that they had been commanded. After these things, Jesus himself commissioned them *to take the message* from the east to the west—the holy and imperishable preaching of eternal salvation. Amen."

b 16:12 Or "to the country." See Luke 24:13–35.

c 16:14 Or "manifested" or "became visible (in clear light)."

will drive out demons in the power of my name. They will speak in tongues. [18]They will be supernaturally protected from snakes and from drinking anything poisonous.[a] And they will lay hands on the sick and heal them."

[19]After saying these things, Jesus was lifted up into heaven and sat down at *the place of honor* at the right hand of God! [20]And the apostles went out announcing the good news everywhere, as the Lord himself consistently worked with them, validating the message they preached with miracle-signs that accompanied them!

---

a 16:18 Or "They will pick up snakes and be unharmed, and whatever poison they drink will not hurt them." Some scholars believe that this sentence contains two Aramaic idioms. To pick up snakes could be a picture of overcoming one's enemies ("snakes"), and drinking poison may be speaking of dealing with attacks on one's character (poisonous words). The imagery is from Psalm 91:13.

About the Translator

Dr. Brian Simmons is known as a passionate lover of God. After a dramatic conversion to Christ, Brian knew that God was calling him to go to the unreached people of the world and present the gospel of God's grace to all who would listen. With his wife, Candice, and their three children, he spent nearly eight years in the tropical rain forest of the Darien Province of Panama as a church planter, translator, and consultant. Brian was involved in the Paya-Kuna New Testament translation project. He studied linguistics and Bible translation principles with New Tribes Mission. After their ministry in the jungle, Brian was instrumental in planting a thriving church in New England (US), and now travels full time as a speaker and Bible teacher. He has been happily married to Candice for over forty-two years and is known to boast regularly of his children and grandchildren. Brian and Candice may be contacted at:

thePassionTranslation.com
Facebook.com/passiontranslation
Twitter.com/tPtBible

For more information about the translation project or any of Brian's books, please visit:

thePassionTranslation.com
StairwayMinistries.org